KEEP IT SIMPLE SELLING

KEEP IT SIMPLE SELLING

The Comprehensive Auto Sales Training Manual

DAMIAN BOUDREAUX

New York

KEEP IT SIMPLE SELLING
The Comprehensive Auto Sales Training Manual

Published in New York, New York, by Morgan James Publishing. Morgan James and The Entrepreneurial Publisher are trademarks of Morgan James, LLC. www.MorganJamesPublishing.com

The Morgan James Speakers Group can bring authors to your live event. For more information or to book an event visit The Morgan James Speakers Group at www.TheMorganJamesSpeakersGroup.com.

A **free** eBook edition is available
with the purchase of this print book.

ISBN 978-1-63047-400-3 paperback
ISBN 978-1-63047-401-0 eBook
Library of Congress Control Number:
2014948647

Interior Design by:
Bonnie Bushman
bonnie@caboodlegraphics.com

CLEARLY PRINT YOUR NAME ABOVE IN UPPER CASE

Instructions to claim your free eBook edition:
1. Download the BitLit app for Android or iOS
2. Write your name in **UPPER CASE** on the line
3. Use the BitLit app to submit a photo
4. Download your eBook to any device

In an effort to support local communities and raise awareness and funds, Morgan James Publishing donates a percentage of all book sales for the life of each book to Habitat for Humanity Peninsula and Greater Williamsburg.

Get involved today, visit
www.MorganJamesBuilds.com

Habitat
for Humanity
Peninsula and
Greater Williamsburg
Building Partner

Keep it Simple Selling is more than just a book.
It's a multimedia training manual. With the purchase of this book,
you also receive the audio book, e-book, downloadable worksheets,
online videos, and access to other auto sales training materials to help
you maximize your productivity and profits in this incredible industry.
All additional materials can be found at
www.AutoTrainingAcademy.com

TABLE OF CONTENTS

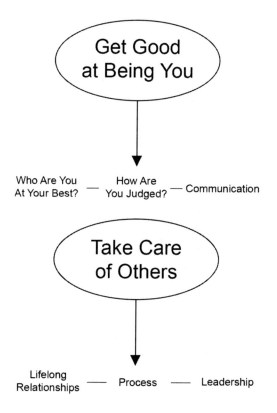

Keep It Simple Success formula

Get good at being you. Take care of others.

Chapter One

THIS BUSINESS
IS A GOLD MINE

"The business of our business is people."

The automotive business is a gold mine. Not just for some. For anyone who wants to reach massive success, it can happen. This industry is incredible. It doesn't matter if you sell cars or trucks or motorcycles. It doesn't matter if you sweep the floors or wash the cars or file paperwork in the office. In this industry, you have the ability to advance as far as you want to. There's no barrier to entry, and there's no glass ceiling. Your raise becomes effective when you do.

There are thousands of success stories out there. Like the kid who started as a driver delivering parts at age 19 and now he's the service director. Or the guy who started out selling motorcycles and is now the general manager of a huge Toyota store. How about the waiter at the restaurant who was invited to sell cars and is now a partner in several dealerships? Or the 16-year-old girl who had to leave high school and get a job because she got pregnant? She started out answering phones and running errands for the office, and now she runs the office, making $250,000 a year. There's also the gentleman who got into this business as a parts picker. He didn't have much education, no high school diploma, and today he's the founder of one of the top dealer groups in the country. There's the used car salesman who is now a mega dealer. And finally, there's the newly-single mother of two who was hired for the Internet department and is now the F&I director. Anything is possible. There are no boundaries.

Or me—Damian Boudreaux. I started out changing oil and washing parts in my friend's transmission shop part time in the evenings. I didn't have any grand ambitions at the time; I was just grateful to have a job so I could pay my rent. Before too long, I became one of the top sellers in the region, and now I train others how to be more successful in sales and in life. *I didn't expect that. I didn't plan for that.* It happened, though. It happened for two reasons: It happened because I figured out who I was and how I could just be myself all the time. And it happened because I started caring more about people than my paycheck.

My mantra for massive success

The business of our business is people. And the key to massive success is *being who you are at your best, and then figuring out how to take care of others.* Master this, and you will be profitable and proud of your way of life.

No matter where you are right now in your life, no matter what your current job is, the key to the future of your dreams lies in mastering who you are at your best, learning how to do your job better than anybody else, and figuring out how to help others. It sounds simple, right? Be yourself. Do a good job. Serve others. Easy. You got this!

So, if it's really that simple, then what's the problem? Why are there so many people failing to achieve the success they desire and deserve? Why aren't you experiencing the massive success you dream of?

The challenges

When I speak to rooms full of salespeople, I hear plenty of reasons why they're not meeting their goals. It starts with the challenge of walking into a different world. When they first start selling cars, they're in a place that's not connectable to anything they've ever related to in their lives. They discover that there are lots of moving parts and different personalities, and the income is uncertain. New salespeople hope and desire and believe they can accomplish something *big.* They have amazing optimism and high expectations. But after a while, they get discouraged. (Sound familiar?) They feel like they're at the mercy of the company's advertising or the economy or other (better) salespeople taking all the good customers.

Some people feel like they don't belong—either in this industry, or at their particular stores. Everyone needs to feel like they belong, like they're part of the family.

There are those who are led to believe that "the less you know, the better off you are." They think the best sales approach is to avoid and evade—saying, "I don't know," or "I can't tell you"—and to believe that buyers are liars.

Some get caught in the fantasy that *everybody else sells their cars cheaper*. They just know the "other guy" is selling for less and giving more for trades. How can they compete? Besides, they tell themselves, "There are too many salespeople on the floor, not enough in stock inventory, and the inventory we have has the wrong equipment."

Salespeople believe that managers are lazy and don't listen. Managers believe that salespeople are lazy and don't do what they're told. Often there's an overarching feeling of favoritism; the house mouse and dealer's pet get the special attention from management.

Salespeople believe that the customers they greet day in and day out don't trust them. They think people immediately judge them as untrustworthy liars. Every person they meet has an accusing look that says, "You're just a salesperson trying to take advantage of me."

Any of this sound familiar to you? It's no wonder salespeople start feeling beat down and frustrated. It's no wonder you feel that you earn very little income compared to the sheer number of hours you work. After all, you've got to eat. You've got to compete with the others on the floor. You face rejection after rejection after rejection, and 80 percent of the people you talk to buy from someone else.

It's like you've got your shoes on the wrong feet. Have you ever done that? Maybe when you were little? Remember how it felt? They hurt; they felt funny. You didn't have to look down—you just knew they didn't fit. That's how the car business can feel. Maybe it's how you feel sometimes. But when everything fits, you feel confident, successful, profitable, and proud. That's my goal for you—to make everything fit perfectly.

Shift your perspective—change your results

I want you to know that all those feelings you're experiencing are normal. Most every salesperson feels them at some time or another. But it's your *perspective* about these challenges that ultimately makes them real or not real. How you look at these challenges determines whether they have control over you. You can choose to continue to ignore them or maybe you'll decide to shift your perspective.

Don't get me wrong. I do NOT want you to change who you are. As you'll soon see, you don't need to change when you know who you are at your best. Instead, you need to embrace, accept, and grow who you are, and that will naturally and easily shift your perspective. You are perfect.

This book is going to teach you how to do just that. It's going to teach you how to succeed in spite of all the challenges. It's going to show you how you can succeed on your terms. If it were up to you, how would you make this business work for you? How could you make this business work for the customer—*and* work for the dealership? How could you make it work in a way that's profitable and lets you be proud of what you do every day? How can it work *naturally*?

The answers to all these questions are the same: get good at being you and serving others, while using a simple process that works for you. This book is probably unlike any sales book you've ever read. It's going to shift your perspective on the business and yourself, so you can get amazing results very quickly.

Question everything

There are so many myths (questionable realities) surrounding our industry. Some of them you may have heard before you even started working as a salesperson. Perhaps you've struggled with some of them for years. We're going to bust these myths wide open during the course of this book. For now, though, see if any of these sound familiar to you.

Questionable Reality #1—The way to sell cars is by waiting for an Up (a sales opportunity). The dealer gives you everything you need to be successful—inventory, service, management support, clerical support, a paycheck, benefits, facilities, phone, advertising, reputation, training, supplies, and location. For some reason, we believe when we come on the showroom floor that the best way to use those resources is to wait for a floor-up, a phone-up, or an Internet lead. Is that creating the profitable, fulfilling career you deserve? Is there a better way than *waiting* to work? How do you accomplish that? Rather than waiting for opportunities, you're going to learn to create a business driven by relationships—where folks visit the dealership to see YOU. The key to success in our great industry is to build and maintain relationships with people who like you and are happy to be with you. We're going to cover how to do this naturally in chapter 6.

Questionable Reality #2—Your competition is external, and you have no control over it. Salespeople tend to feel they are competing against external forces like other salespeople, other dealerships, better advertising, the economy, other brands, the used car manager, and F&I. How do you succeed when at times these forces seem to be pitted against you? How do you succeed in spite of them? The truth is, your greatest competition lives within yourself. You're actually competing against your own self-talk and your perception of those external forces. Don't focus on the competition. Choosing to be negatively influenced by your competition is a recipe for hunger, anxiety, and a business that is less than fulfilling. Focus on you at your best—and taking care of people. That'll make you profitable and proud. We'll discuss this in chapter 3.

Questionable Reality #3—Asking for referrals! Dealers spend ridiculous amounts of money to teach salespeople things they're not naturally going to do. Is it a good idea to ask for referrals? Yes. Does it happen on a regular basis? No. Folks even quote scripture as proof; the Bible says *ask* (for referrals) *and you shall receive* (referrals). Yet still, we rarely do it. The reason is because salespeople will do more for someone else than they will normally do for themselves. Getting referrals needs to be about asking and *giving*. Bring more value into your customers' lives. Do more and sell more. You'll discover some great ways to do this in chapter 6.

Questionable Reality #4—The House Mouse gets all the best cheese. I used to believe the top salespeople were the ones who got all the house deals. We called a person like this the House Mouse. But kneeling down and begging for the crumbs your managers give you is no way to succeed. You want to be the "Back-of-the-House" Mouse, basing your success on relationships with *everyone* in the dealership, not just the manager who happens to get a few leads. We'll talk about this in chapter 6.

Questionable Reality #5—Managers yell. *Managers do not yell.* Many of them are just communication challenged. Consider this: when talking at a high volume using only one note, it comes across as yelling. If your manager would simply add a little melody to the volume, it comes across totally differently. When the yelling begins, the teaching ends. If you're in this business, you probably communicate pretty well already. However, by the time you finish this book, you'll know what it takes to be a truly excellent communicator. Plus, you'll be better able to read your customers' body language and non-verbal communication, too. Chapter 5 is all about learning to become a great communicator.

Questionable Reality #6—The road to the sale. You must memorize, learn, and understand your 12-step selling process, or 10 steps to the sale, or however many steps your dealership has. Here's a little secret for you—salespeople who have been in the business for 25 years still can't list, recite, or write down the road to the sale easily. The sales process works, but it's unnatural. It's not based on behaviors you've been doing your whole life. So how do you get your selling process to be highly effective, simple, memorable, and based on natural behavior? That's what you're going to learn in chapter 7.

Questionable Reality #7—Training starts with learning word tracks. Only 7 percent of communication is about words, while 93 percent of communication involves how you bring those words to life. Yet many in our industry spend as much as 70 percent of sales training covering the 7 percent of the words we use to communicate. If you're going to be worth listening to, doesn't it make sense to engage the other 93 percent of our communication skills when we are learning? Managers are taught to "load your lips"—focusing on the words you're going to say. What you need to master is how to load your whole body before you go and ask for the sale. Have you ever heard someone say, "You sound like a car salesman"? We come across as a bunch of parrots, all sounding the same. Some of us talk like this when we're not even at work; we might be at a bar or a function with our kids. Are we supposed to all sound alike? I didn't sound like a car salesman in high school. What happened? Be worth listening to; be compelling, powerful, and a brilliant communicator. We'll look at lots of different ways to communicate more powerfully in chapter 5.

Questionable Reality #8—Proud of what—30 day trophies? What motivates you? Trips, cash-in-fist contests, a paycheck, recognition, awards, bonuses, a new boat, a fancier car, a bigger house? Now, what about your business makes you proud and drives you every day? When you find that reason to be proud of what you do every day, then your sense of accomplishment is driven by your mission. When that happens, your numbers will explode effortlessly. I'll tell you a cool story about this in chapter 8.

Questionable Reality #9—Beginner's luck to getting your dealer's license. Success to struggle—I know you've seen this one. Many salespeople come in, and for the first 90 days or so, they're selling everyone. Then for some reason, their sales just start to drop off. Why? Is it because they don't know anything? Is it a lack of knowledge or training? Why do sales drop off? It's because when they start, they believe every customer will buy. When they get farther along, however, they stop believing everyone is going to buy. When people first start selling cars, they're full of what we call hopeium (the opium of hope). They are hungry, and they need this to work out, so they are carried by the intoxicating waves of hopeium. They don't know anything except to be themselves, be authentic, and get people into the best cars they can. The more they learn and experience in the day-to-day sales world, they see things begin to change. If their sales drop, it's usually because they moved away from simplicity and authenticity, they stopped believing in the deal, and they discovered the negative in each opportunity. The good news is, each of these components is 100 percent in your control. You can have beginner's luck every single day of your life, and you're about to learn how.

The top salespeople learn to question the "myths" of their businesses and operate from a more efficient perspective. If you have any of these defeating beliefs carved in stone in your heart, it might take some time and real-world proof to chip them away. If you're skeptical, I get it. I've been there. But once I experienced my life (and my paycheck) through my new perspective, I never looked back. The changes were so dramatic, I wanted to shout it from the rooftops. If you consistently apply what you learn in this book, you're going to start seeing similar dramatic changes. Get ready for it—your life is going to blow your mind!

What most sales trainings teach

There are strategies I teach in this book that are unlike anything you've ever heard in a classroom or sales program before. Most sales trainings in the auto industry teach the Xs and Os from the playbook. They teach strategies and tactics and word scripts and 10-step processes. All of that stuff is great. It does work. A lot of time and energy goes into those trainings. But often they are not easy and don't make sense. It's a struggle for you to be who you are at your best. For some salespeople, it works fine. But for so many of us, it's too complicated and doesn't come naturally. Often the traditional sales trainings don't work because they ask you to change who you are. You don't need to change who you are. Who you are is just perfect!

You see, those trainings are focusing on *your* needs. *You* need to make more sales and more money. So *you* need to memorize more scripts and work a better process. But that's backward. What you really need to be doing is focusing on what the *customer* needs, then what you can do to help. The business of our business is people. I'm serious when I say this business is a gold mine. But you have to drill down to get to that vein of gold. Once you're there, you have to stay there and expand and grow.

I teach something different

Imagine for a moment how it would feel if all you had to do to sell cars was be yourself and find ways to serve others naturally and easily. How would your life be different if opportunities continuously dropped out of the sky and into your lap, with less stress or struggle? If you never had to verbally talk to a customer from a memorized script or struggle to remember your 10-step process again, would that be okay with you? *Think YES* if you'd like your world to be that simple and natural.

This book digs deeper than traditional sales programs or books. We're going to start by finding out who you are at your best. Because when you work in harmony with what's already inside you, everything becomes simple. I'm going to walk you through a series of exercises to discover who you are deep down. What's the authentic you? Each person is unique. Who you are at your best is not the same as who I am at my best. So don't skip this step! Even if it sounds a little strange, do it anyway. Complete the exercises honestly, and privately. This is about discovering who *you are*, not who someone else thinks you should be. Once you discover who you are at your best, you're going to learn some strategies for getting really good at being who you are all the time. Don't be surprised when this discovery process improves more than just your sales. It can improve every aspect of your life, if you want it to.

Getting good at you

Once you know who you are at your best, you're going to learn how to be that person all the time. This is all about discovering how to use the characteristics and values you *already possess* inside yourself to connect with others in a meaningful way. These are not the characteristics that your parents, teachers, friends, or bullies assigned to you when you were young. (Those are nothing more than external labels you can peel off anytime you choose to.) You are going to look inside yourself and recognize your own unique brilliance. We'll examine your strengths and your weaknesses. Not everyone has the same qualities they are naturally good at, so we'll determine the things you might want to avoid. It's easier to move toward your strengths and away from your weaknesses when you actually know what they are. For example, I'm great at telling stories and entertaining groups. Nobody gives a sales meeting like me! But ask me to organize my desk or calendar, and you can forget it. It's never going to happen. I'm terrible at organization. But that's okay. I've learned how to be successful in spite of my disorganization. The point is, I know this about myself.

Getting good at you is also about learning how people judge you, and how to make sure both you and your company maintain an impeccable reputation. To do that, we'll set up three simple rules of engagement that work for you, for your customers, and for your company. Whenever you have to make a decision, you'll be able to apply these rules and know immediately which direction will yield the best results.

Finally, getting good at you is about learning to communicate at an extremely high level. Only about 7 percent of communication is words. Yet that seems to be all we study in typical sales training. After years of study, I've learned that the other 93 percent of communication is how you bring the words to life, and how you interpret the words other people say (or don't say). You're going to learn strategies to help you communicate better—with your customers, with your manager, with your neighbors, with everyone. After all, if the business of our business is people, the better you communicate with people, the more money you'll make.

Caring for others—Building and maintaining lifelong relationships

The second half of this perspective shift is dedicated to serving others by building and maintaining lifelong relationships. Anyone can build relationships; that's not difficult. But the very best salespeople build *and maintain* relationships that last a lifetime. That's their big secret. Throughout the second part of this book, you're going to see why the way you sell cars now may be inefficient and downright crazy. And you'll discover how to get out of the "waiting for Ups" business and get into the "relationship" business. After all, that's where the easy money is.

This is all about caring for others—not just people who might buy from you, but *all* people. Imagine what your world might be like if you treated everyone like royalty. You're going to learn how to grow your income by building and maintaining relationships, instead of waiting around for the next Up (or sales opportunity). The business of our business is people; that's the key. If you can build and maintain and grow relationships, you will have lifelong success in an industry that will reward you and promote you to a level you can't even imagine.

Once you've got the hang of expanding your relationships in a way that brings you more business, we're going to dive into the only sales process you'll ever need. The last "road to the sale" you'll ever have to learn. It's a three-step process that distills every other sales process (you know, the 8 or 10 or 12-step ones) down into the most basic components. The best part is, you've been doing this process your whole life, so you already know how to do it! You just need a little guidance to see how to apply it to selling cars. You'll learn that in chapter 7.

Finally, we're going to discuss leadership. Maybe you're a manager or a dealer right now. Maybe you'd like to be a manager or a dealer someday. Either way, we're going to take a look at how managers, dealers, and owners can use the information in this book to lead and inspire their salespeople, techs, office team, and everyone in the dealership to perform their jobs better. After all, the better they all do their jobs, the more money everyone makes.

Who is this Boudreaux guy?

I know something about you. I know that before you'll listen to me or learn what I want to show you, you have to know something about me.

I got into this business because I was two months behind on my rent and nobody else would hire me. My friend hired me to clean parts at his transmission shop at night, and I was so grateful. I would go to work every night cleaning transmission parts, and I loved it. He and I got to be good friends. After about 60 days, he decided it might be better if I sold cars. I have no idea where he came up with that idea, but he opened up a used car lot and put me in charge. It was called Broad Street Auto Sales, and it only took about 4 months for him to fire me. There was no way I was qualified to run a business, it's just not in my nature.

I needed to get another job. So I went down the street to the local Chevrolet store, and they hired me to change oil. Exactly 30 days later, the owner sold the dealership. The new owner knew my family and was happy to see me there, and for some crazy reason, he decided I should sell cars. He said he would pay me minimum wage for as many hours as I wanted to work. Now let me tell you, I can work some hours! I'm not afraid to work. I'll work 80 hours a week, if I can. They also gave me a little Cavalier to drive, so I didn't have to drive that old Mercury anymore. I had a brand new car! I was so excited to get to work, and I talked to everyone I knew. That first paycheck, I made $1,600. I was rich! I paid off my back rent. I bought my future ex-wife some flowers. And I got a manicure because I'd always wanted to have one.

I called my dad and told him I was going to be rich. I had never seen $1,600 in my whole life. And that started my journey selling automobiles.

Remember that myth about beginner's luck? I slammed into it like it was a brick wall. I watched people, and I learned. I became a serious student of the car sales business. As hard as I tried, and as many hours as I worked, I was stuck between 7 to 12 cars a month. Now you might think, that's not so bad. But it is bad when there are people at the dealership selling 20 to 25 cars every month. I compared myself to them and thought *what do they have that I don't? Why are they better than me?*

It wasn't always like that. There were some months where I was almost salesman of the month. Of course, the next month I was almost fired. Then the next, I was almost salesman of the month again. I went up and down and up and down. It was frustrating, and I was exhausted!

This was 1983. The world was different then. There was no Internet. People would come to the dealership with a copy of *Consumer Reports* in their hands and spend forever looking at prices and trying to figure out the cost. We would go home every night and pray for an easier, faster way to do our jobs. Back then, we had 14 percent unemployment in Lake Charles, Louisiana. But thank goodness we had great interest rates, because someone with incredible credit qualified for F&I's Preferred Rate of 17.95 percent. My friends qualified for 26 percent to 32 percent interest, and they were grateful that the state capped interest at 32 percent because Texas was even higher. That was the world we lived in. If you were going to wait for an Up in South Louisiana, you were going to starve to death, because nobody came in the store. I knew something wasn't right, but I didn't know what.

After a year and a half, I had had enough of the struggling. I decided that my problem was simple geography. I was in the wrong town. So, I moved to Houston, Texas. It was a two and a half hour drive from home, and nobody knew who I was. You know what's great about nobody knowing who you are? You can become anyone you want! In two and a half hours, I became a college graduate. I told everyone there that I was a college graduate; I was looking to build the sense of significance I thought I needed in the real world. I lied to everyone, and for the first three weeks, I didn't sell a single car. I was miserable. I knew in my heart I wasn't supposed to be there. So, I went to my general sales manager and said, "This is not for me."

He said I was good. He said I could do this. He said he had my back. "Just go talk to people, Boudreaux," he said. So, I went back to the floor, and sure enough, I started selling some cars. There were a couple of months I sold 16 to 18 cars. My God, I was rich! But still, there were those months when I was almost fired. It was like the roller coaster ride all over again.

The worst part was, I knew I was better. I had this number in my head—26 cars. I'm supposed to sell 26. But you can't sell 26, if you can't break 20. So 20 became my Roger Banister "moment." If I could only break 20, then I could get to 26. So, I busted my butt. I talked to everybody. I was running to greet people, and I thought, *you're not going to outrun me!* Sure enough, on the 20th of the month, I had 16 cars. I thought, *I got this. It's finally going to happen.*

And as soon as I thought *I got it*, a great big invisible Sabotage Button appeared out of nowhere, and I pressed it. I blew my success to smithereens! F&I helped by kicking back three perfectly good deals for some crazy reason. My managers were yelling at me for something I didn't have anything to do with this time. My future ex-wife was yelling at me for forgetting to take the garbage out on Thursday. I don't even remember when Thursday is…and, anyway, you cooked the garbage, *you* take it out! And thank goodness I got a toothache. Where'd that come from? I'd never had a toothache before—that's crazy.

I ended up with 18 cars for the month. My business was up and down, survival to almost successful. This was supposed to be *my month.*

I was miserable. I was frustrated. I was angry. And I was done. That's it. I'M IN THE WRONG BUSINESS! There's no other explanation. It's supposed to be easier. In this dealership, there were 6 other people selling more than 26 cars a month. And they were no better than me. I just couldn't figure out what they were doing differently. Maybe they were getting all the house deals, and the managers were feeding them solid. But one guy sold 40 cars a month, and he wasn't any better than me. I quit!

Only my manager wouldn't let me quit. He believed in me and said I just needed to take some time off because I was too emotional. He said I should go back to Louisiana and go hunting or fishing or cooking or whatever it was we do back there. Then if I came back and still wanted to quit, he would let me quit.

So I did. I took a leave of absence, and I went home. I drove two and a half hours back to Lake Charles, and I saw the world I grew up in totally differently. For the first time, I saw my home and my family from the outside. I could look at it more objectively because I had been away. I went to my dad's drug store and really watched him for the first time. Now, my family had owned the drug store since 1923, and I had been working there since I was a kid. But for some reason, I saw something new this time.

I watched my dad and my Uncle Jerry as they loved and cared for patients. If you couldn't afford your medicine, your medicine was free. They were not there to sell cough syrup or a prescription. They were there to *solve people's health needs.* They were not attached to the money. They were attached to the customer's' good health. They were mission driven. My eyes opened wide and I felt like I'd just seen the sun after living a year underground. I watched them treat people like royalty. They weren't *selling* anything; they were *solving problems.* And I thought, *that should be me.* I hated selling. People would say, "Boudreaux could sell ice cream to Eskimos." But I didn't want to sell ice cream to Eskimos; they probably wanted hot chocolate.

As I continued to watch, I saw that Dad had a sales process. He didn't know it, but he had one. Now I knew all about sales processes, because in the car business you have to learn the 12 steps (or 10 steps or 8 steps or whatever). Here's the challenge: I could never remember all the steps. They had the steps all over the conference room. They put 'em on my desk. But I still couldn't remember them. My manager would say I was unprofessional or I wasn't committed to my profession. I thought that was crazy. I knew I was committed and wanted to be successful. I wanted to make it! It was just too hard to remember all those steps.

My dad's process was brilliant. He didn't even know he had it. When the front door opened and someone walked in, he would stop what he was doing and say, "Hi Cuz! How you doin'?" (My dad called everybody "Cuz," because he couldn't remember anyone's name—not even the names of his seven children.)

The customer would say, "Mr. Robert, I'm not feeling good."

Dad would walk over and ask the customer a bunch of questions to get a picture of what was going on with the man's health. He'd ask, "Do you have a temperature? Are you achy? What about your nose? Is it stuffy? Are you coughing? Do you have a sore throat?" He would keep asking questions and listening to the answers until he got the picture of what was going on with this customer's health. I watched this and thought, *oh my God, he's doing the first five steps!* He did the greet, built rapport, the wants/needs analysis, qualified the customer—all of it. He did everything that we do in five steps, but Dad did it in one step.

I wasn't in the wrong business. I was in this business wrong.

I learned a lot more from my father during my time back home. When I finally went back to Houston, I decided I was going to try selling the way he did. I was going to talk to people and be 100 percent present with them. I was going to ask questions until I got the picture about what they wanted or needed. *And I was going to care more about the people than the money.* I wish I could tell you that a switch flipped in my head and I figured it all out instantaneously, but it didn't. It took a little more time for me to put all the pieces together. But when I got back to Houston, I did sell more cars. And it didn't take long before I blew past my 26 car goal and started selling 30, 40, 60 cars a month. My best month was 102 cars, but after I realized what I was doing and how all the pieces fit together, I never sold fewer than 28 cars a month ever again.

Maybe you're like me. You want to be successful. You want the shiny car and the big house and the awesome bank account. You want your family to be secure, and you want the freedom of having your own business. You want to be proud of what you do. But you don't have those things. You don't have that feeling. You're struggling. And you just want to figure out how to make the process work.

Here's the great news

Because you're reading this book, you get to shortcut the learning process. You don't have to go through months or years of figuring it all out. By the time you read to the end, if you complete the exercises and really implement what I teach you, you're going to know the secrets of the top salespeople. You'll be able to take your sales to new heights and reap rewards you never dreamed possible. Best of all, you'll be proud of what you do.

How to get the most out of this book

What's your book-reading personality? Are you a front-to-back reader who never cheats or looks ahead to find out if your favorite character is still alive? Or are you a skipper-arounder—you know, someone who likes to start reading in random places every time you open the book?

No matter which way you like to read, you will be happy with this book. If you like to read beginning to end, great! But if you prefer, you can jump around a bit. Each chapter is written to stand on its own.

If you just read the chapter about how others judge you, you will get something out of it. If you just read about the Keep It Simple Selling three-step process, you'll get something out of it. Each chapter holds a stand-alone concept; each is important on its own. However, please be sure to read the next chapter, "Getting The Picture," first. Once you have that as a foundation, everything else will make sense.

This book is a three-dimensional multimedia training experience. Literally. Some of the concepts and strategies that I teach are best learned by watching them in action. So, I've set up a special section on my website just for you. From time to time, I will ask you to log in to a certain web address and watch a video or listen to an audio or download an exercise. Please don't skip these. Salespeople have made a lot of money using these techniques. They will blow your mind! To access this special training, you will need to log in with your name and email. If you're reading this on an iPad or another electronic reader, all you have to do is click the link. If you are reading the physical book, you will need to get online somehow—on your computer or on your phone. Don't miss out on these opportunities. When it's time to go online, do it.

Keep an open mind

I want you to know that the Keep It Simple Selling process you're going to learn works equally well for whatever profession you're in. It works whether you're selling cars or motorcycles or boats or toothpaste. It also has applications for your health, wealth, and relationships. You can take this book and read it from the perspective of improving relationships with employees, family, and friends. Don't view this as just another sales strategy—incorporate it into your life, and it will improve overall.

Finally, understand that this process might take some practice. Some of it will make immediate sense, and you will start to incorporate it unconsciously. In my experience working with thousands of salespeople, I've discovered that once you give your brain permission to think in a new way, you will naturally start behaving differently. It's great if you get it right away. But it's also great if you need to work on it for a while. As you will soon see, all of the concepts you're going to learn are based on natural human behavior, so you will get it eventually.

Practice. Make it yours. Be yourself, and great things will happen.

Let's get started.

Chapter Two

GET THE PICTURE

"Get The Picture to discover the PP."

Get The Picture—it's something you've been doing your whole life, whether you realize it or not. Remember going on a date with someone for the first time? If you're like most people, you spent a lot of time on that date asking questions. You may have even researched them on the web. *What do they do for a living? What kind of food do they like? What kind of food don't they like? Do they have any brothers and sisters? Where did they grow up? Did they like it there? Do they have any pets?* All of these questions are designed to give you a picture about that person so you can relate to them better. (Because you're building a relate-tionship.)

Remember applying for a job? You probably filled out a resume and answered a lot of questions to give the HR department an amazing picture of who you were and what you were great at doing. Then if you went in for an interview, you answered more questions to give them a more detailed picture of who you were.

How about buying gifts for others? *Do they like chocolates? What's their favorite brand of chocolate? Do they prefer truffles or fudge? Filled or unfilled? Oh, they prefer jewelry? Well, do they like necklaces or earrings? Pendants or bracelets?* You probably ask some questions to Get The Picture of what they like best before you make your decision.

The longer you're in a relationship with someone, the better the picture you'll develop. Knowing which restaurant to choose for a romantic anniversary dinner is probably easier than knowing which one to choose for your first date. You probably don't have to ask your significant other what kind of food she likes because you already have that picture.

Getting The Picture is about building certainty. It's about making sure you understand people or situations thoroughly, so you can better understand who they are, what they're about, and what challenges or opportunities they present. Get The Picture is about curiosity and discovery; it helps bring clarity. It's about assessing, sizing things up, and judging for yourself how to serve people, solve problems, or accomplish something new and exciting.

It's all about the "PP"

I mean it—everything. If you've ever been in any kind of relationship, you got into it or out of it because of your PP. You're reading this book right now because of your PP. You went on your first date and your last job interview because of your PP. Your next customer is going to talk to you because of their PP. It doesn't matter who you are; it's all about the PP. It runs the world.

There are two major reasons people do things—to move away from a *Problem* or to move toward a *Possibility.* That's the PP—Problems and Possibilities.

This is why we do things. You're reading this book right now because you may want to move away from the Problem of your paycheck and/or move toward the Possibility (and probability) of greater wealth and abundance. You got married because you wanted to move away from the Problem of being single and lonely on Friday nights and move toward the Possibility of an incredible lifelong relationship. Your customer buys a new vehicle from you to move away from the Problem of her older vehicle, and to move toward the Possibility of a vehicle she can be proud to drive.

When you ask questions, you Get The Picture in order to discover the PP. The reason for discovering the PP is so you can better solve a customer's transportation needs. Great salespeople ask questions to Get The Picture and discover PP. Once you know the PP, you can use it as leverage to influence people to take action now. Making a sale doesn't have to be about dropping the monthly payment by $20. It's about knowing that person just got a new job and is embarrassed to drive his older vehicle to the office. It's about knowing that Mom just got into a wreck with her babies in the car, and she needs a vehicle she feels safe and confident driving. It's about discovering what people *really want* and then helping them get it.

Get The Picture is the first step in selling, solving, or serving

When selling cars, the first thing you want to do is get the customer's picture. For example, find out what they're currently driving. Specifically, you can ask:

- What are you currently driving?
- Did you buy it new or previously enjoyed?
- How long have you had it?
- When is your next payment due?
- How much are your payments?
- How did you get your payment so low?
- What do you like best about your vehicle?
- What else do you like about it?
- What else?
- What do you like least about your vehicle?
- What else don't you like about it?
- What else?

These questions have been taught in our industry for a long time, and with good reason. What hasn't been taught is *why* these are great questions. They are great questions to "Get The Picture" about what the customer is currently driving. Knowing what they're currently driving helps you know more about their P.P. Problems and/or Possibilities. Every question adds to the picture.

For example, "When's your next payment due?"

- You might discover that the customer is late on their payments, or early, or maybe the bill is about to come due and that amount could be used as a down payment.

"What do you like most about what you're currently driving?" What else? What else?"

- This might tell you what the Possibilities are, and what values they have in their current vehicle that are important to them in the next vehicle.

"What don't you like about your current vehicle?" What else? What else?"

- This may tell you about the Problems the customer is moving away from. Maybe she doesn't like the gas mileage, or the fact that it was in a wreck two weeks ago and now has a strange sound coming from the engine, or that it belonged to her ex-husband. There are lots of things a customer could dislike like about this vehicle, and it's your job to find them all out as part of Getting The Picture.

"Who else drives the vehicle?"

"Who else rides in the vehicle? Kids? Spouse? Critters?"

"Do they take any special trips?"

"Do they haul anything with the vehicle?

"Do they have any hobbies they need the vehicle for?"

All these questions help you Get The Picture about how they use their current vehicle. Next, you'll want to ask questions about what Possibilities they're hoping for in the next vehicle. These help narrow down the choices so that you can introduce the customer to the lowest priced, in stock unit that fits their picture.

We're going to talk about Get The Picture throughout this book. The important thing to understand is that you've been doing this your whole life. You already know how to do it. You're an expert! I'm going to show you how to tap into your inner expert and how to apply your natural behavior to the car business—and leverage it to help you sell more cars and have a career you are proud of.

Own it!

It's time for you to implement what you've learned so far. I want this information to come so easily to you that you can't help but live it every day. Please don't skip this section. Answer the questions below and definitely WRITE IN THE BOOK. Do it!

No one's watching!

Ask _____ to Get The Picture.

You Get The Picture to discover the ___.

PP stands for _____and _____.

We make decisions to move away from _____ and toward _____.

*Bonus—

We ask questions to " _____ ____ _____ " and discover the " ___ "!!!

BREAK THE RULES...WRITE IN THE BOOK!

_____
_____
_____
_____
_____
_____
_____
_____
_____
_____
_____
_____
_____
_____
_____
_____
_____
_____
_____
_____
_____
_____
_____
_____
_____

Chapter Three

WHO YOU ARE AT YOUR BEST

"Let me introduce you to someone amazing!"

One of the most important things you can ever discover in your life is who you are at your best. People pay hundreds of thousands of dollars in education, therapy, and coaching trying to find the answer to the question, *Who am I?* They will spend years of their lives wandering curiously from place to place, job to job, relationship to relationship—all trying to "find themselves." They are led to believe that if they could just change *this* about themselves or *that* about themselves, then life would be easier and more rewarding. Most of them never do find themselves or manage to change. It seems like such a simple question, yet they often never get an answer. Why is this?

The reason why they rarely get the answers is they're looking in the wrong places. You can spend your entire life searching the whole world for your true self—who you're meant to be—and you'll rarely find it out there. Not in a hundred lifetimes.

You see, the answer isn't *out there*. Most of the time, it's *inside of us*. Who you are begins by looking *inside* and accepting yourself.

Now what does this have to do with selling cars? Everything! The key to massive success in this business is creating and maintaining lifelong relationships. That means you have to care for and serve others. And you cannot fully care for and serve others with your best self until you know who you are at your best—and until you get good at being that person every day.

Once you master what I'm about to teach, you're going to notice your whole life shifting to a better place. You'll do better at work, sure—but you'll also notice you have better relationships with your loved ones. You'll start to pay more attention to your health. All sorts of things improve when you learn who you are at your best, and then you apply the right qualities and characteristics you *already possess* to every endeavor in your life.

Let me introduce you to someone amazing

Right now, I'm going to pull back the curtain and introduce you to the most incredible person in the world—YOU! This is awesome—are you ready?

In this section, you'll see a list of blank lines labeled, "Who I am at my best." On this page, I want you to take just a couple of minutes and very quickly write down a list of words that describe you at your best. I know you know this. It's already inside you. These words should be adjectives—positive, descriptive words. They should not be, "I am a great mom" or "I am a good dad." You want single descriptive words. And remember, this is who you are *at your best*—not necessarily how you're feeling right now.

I am all about challenging rules. So I want you to know you can write in this book. This isn't grade school, and the teacher isn't looking over your shoulder. Don't analyze. Just do it. Do not skip this part. Do not just think it up in your head. We're going to work with this list throughout the rest of this book, and you're going to want the words in front of you. If you really can't bring yourself to write in the book, you can go to http://AutoTrainingAcademy.com/i-am-characteristics/ and download the I AM Worksheet to use. (If you're going to use the worksheet, go get it now.)

Write down as many positive qualities, characteristics, and values of WHO YOU ARE, AT YOUR BEST. Use the powerful words I AM in front of each word. See if you can get to 60.

Here are some examples:

I AM <u>smart</u>.

I AM <u>kind</u>.

I AM <u>happy</u>.

Okay. Go!

I AM _____   I AM _____

I AM _____   I AM _____

I AM _____   I AM _____

I AM _____   I AM _____

I AM _____   I AM _____

I AM _____   I AM _____

I AM _____   I AM _____
I AM _____   I AM _____
I AM _____   I AM _____
I AM _____   I AM _____
I AM _____   I AM _____
I AM _____   I AM _____
I AM _____   I AM _____
I AM _____   I AM _____
I AM _____   I AM _____
I AM _____   I AM _____
I AM _____   I AM _____
I AM _____   I AM _____
I AM _____   I AM _____
I AM _____   I AM _____
I AM _____   I AM _____
I AM _____   I AM _____
I AM _____   I AM _____
I AM _____   I AM _____
I AM _____   I AM _____
I AM _____   I AM _____
I AM _____   I AM _____
I AM _____   I AM _____
I AM _____   I AM _____

How impressive are you? You are brilliant!

Did you fill up all the blanks? Or did you stop? It doesn't matter if you made it all the way to 60 or if you stopped at 20. What you've just done is answer the question all of humanity is asking all the time—*who am I?* (And it didn't cost you thousands of dollars or years of your life!)

I want you to see where your true identity comes from. How do you know who you are? Does it come from outside you? You know, all those people who told you who you were when you were younger— unfriendly children on the playground, unsupportive parents, confused and overwhelmed teachers? Do you let external forces and people define who you are and how you behave?

Here's how I got my identity for my whole childhood. I was born with dark circles under my eyes, and the kids used to call me "Raccoon." I didn't like that. That was not me. But the other children said it was. Until I was six years old, I sucked my finger like a baby. It did terrible things to my teeth, so they called me "Snaggle Tooth" and "Bucky." I hated being Bucky! I wasn't Bucky; I was Damian.

It was like every time kids called me one of those names, they had a label—with knives on the back—and they stuck that label on me and the knives plunged into my chest. It hurt. I didn't want to be those names. So thank God, in sixth grade, I was playing football one day. I went out for a pass. I looked back to see the ball. I stretched out my hands…and the ball went right through them. Thank God for that day, because now they could call me Butterfingers. And when they got tired of that, they made fun of my last name. They called me Buttroll, instead of Boudreaux. Labels. Stuck on me from the outside. Labels I hated, but I didn't know how to change them.

How did people label you when you were younger? Smart? Funny? Crazy? Ugly? Fat? Skinny? Pizza Face?

And how did it feel?

Now, I didn't have it bad. It wasn't like kids have it today. I work closely with elementary school children, and in my work, I often see little fourth grade girls labeled as fat, as dumb, as ugly. They feel like they don't belong. And I see kids with parents who love them, but still call them *stupid* or *brat*. Those kids wonder what they did wrong, and promise they'll do better—just to please a parent. It's heartbreaking! These kids have their whole worlds shattered, and if they don't change course, they'll forever look at themselves through little shards of broken glass trying to figure out who they are. And it will be tragically difficult for them to pick up all the pieces, fit them together, smooth out the cracks, and see themselves as whole, wonderful people.

But you see, a bully doesn't have any effect on a child (or an adult) with a great sense of identity—a sense of identity that comes from the *inside*. When someone knows who they are, those labels just don't stick. My little girl started at a new school, and one of the other girls called her *ugly*. Nichole's response was simply, "Dad, obviously she's blind!" Nichole knows who she is on the inside, and when it doesn't match the labels people try to put on her, she has the power to simply know *that's not me*. It's not the truth about her, so she can ignore it. And that external force (or person) has no power over her. They called my daughter, Anna Louise, dumb because of the way she talked. But Anna's a *genius*, and she knew it. The label meant nothing to her, so it had no sting.

That's what I want for you. I want you to define and know who you really are—so that any words you hear that don't align with your definition don't take hold in your ears. That's what this list you created is—your true identity. It's who you are on the inside. And it's critical that you know who that person is, even if you don't always feel like that person right now.

So who are you?

Whether you realize it or not, you've been trying to figure this out your whole life. You've been in an internal conflict, trying to figure out what's going on and where you fit in the world. You know you want to be good. You know you want to be happy. You know you want to be profitable. You definitely want to be proud of who you are and what you do. How in the world do you get there?

You get there by being who you are at your best every day, consistently, and then going out and serving others by solving their Problems or helping them get what they need or desire.

It will be difficult to successfully help and serve others until you look in the mirror and know your brilliance—*and* what you suck at. Really knowing yourself—finally acknowledging your strengths and weaknesses—is critical to getting what you desire in life.

And it's a piece of inner-work that most sales trainers skip over. Either because they don't know how to do the work, or because they don't comprehend the connection between knowing who you are at your best and selling more cars. There is a strong connection! It goes far deeper than selling cars, too. Knowing who you are at your best is the *foundation* for getting whatever you want in life. Whether you want excellent health, a rocking love life, the career of your dreams, boatloads of money, happy relationships, mental and spiritual growth—it doesn't matter *what you want*, the key is knowing *who you are*.

Now, I know there might be a part of you that wants to skip this step. It's a little "woo-woo" and part of you deep down might think this is just too weird. Why do you have to know who you are to sell cars? Why can't you just memorize the newest, super-duper word tracks? Please trust yourself and allow me to lead you through a few short exercises in self-exploration. You will be rewarded beyond your wildest imagination. Can you do that for yourself? (Smile and think, "yes.")

What's distracting you from success?

Be aware of your competition. I'm not talking about the dealer down the street, or even the top sales guy at your company. I want you to see what are you competing against every day. Whether you realize it or not, you're competing against distractions that come into your life from every direction all the time. Maybe you wake up in the morning and the first thing you do before you even go to the bathroom is look at Facebook or your email. Now, don't get me wrong. Facebook is good. But is it *that* good? You get an email at 4 o'clock in the morning and you actually go answer it. It's crazy. The worst is when you're sitting at work and you're distracted by the game of solitaire on your computer. For some people, the computer is the most expensive deck of cards ever invented.

You're competing against all kinds of distractions on a daily basis, and you're not even aware of it. What are your distractions? What's keeping you from being productive at your job, from being present with your family, from enjoying your friends and activities that make you happy? What tools and strategies do you use to help you procrastinate? What's keeping you from experiencing the growth you are so hungry for in your life? That growth might be spiritual or financial or in your relationships—it doesn't matter. You have to become aware of the distractions that get in your way.

I am a student of Brendon Burchard. Brendon teaches that an email, phone call, or text message is actually a summons for you to pay attention to other people's agendas. They're all just other people's agendas being forced on you and competing for your attention. Your job, your life, is much more important than their agendas. Own your agenda!

You might be competing against your family—whether they are horrible, or whether you're so in love with them that you want to be part of their lives every single day. Their drama becomes your drama. Your family controls the outcomes of your world. You have no control over your world because your family tells you what to do—good or bad. You surrendered control to someone else.

How about your boss? Maybe a part of you is saying that the reason you can't succeed at work is because your manager is mean to you. He talks down to you and doesn't give you the support you need. Why are you choosing to let him control your feelings? Why is he the one who says how you should feel today? Why are you trying to figure out a way to make him like you, so you can do better at work? Here's a little hint: the corporation is not the problem. You've got to find a way to be happy and productive *in spite* of the corporation. Or *in spite* of the manager who, for some crazy reason, hates your guts. You can't be competing with your boss.

Some people are competing with the media. Tragedy! Horrific! Things are terrible! Worry about this right now! We could all DIE!!!! In 15 minutes, the media can control your attention for the whole day. You go spinning out of control into a tizzy of worry and fear and insanity. You're letting them run your whole life. You base your prospects for success on who's in office—Democrats or Republicans. The media has you chanting, *If only we could get a Democrat, then we could be successful. Now we got a Democrat—thank goodness! Now we can be successful. Oh, man, I'm still not doing so good. If only we could get a Republican in office…* Then the cycle starts all over again with the other side. Listen to me; it doesn't matter if you're kneeling down behind a donkey or an elephant, you're still going to get crapped on by an animal! Do you see how crazy this is? You're letting someone else—someone outside of you—control whether or not you're successful. It doesn't make any sense.

No matter what your favorite media distraction is, it's all a sideshow. The main show is YOU. It's time you started paying attention to the person in the mirror. You are the one who makes the difference, not all those other distractions you're letting control you. Don't feel too bad, though; the media are experts at manipulating your attention. It's how they survive. They are really, really good at controlling you, and sliding you into your survival instincts. Once you're aware of it, though, you can begin to see how they do it, and release yourself from the media grip.

What about your friends? Are they distractions, too? Do you have friends who suck you dry, drag you down with their negativity, behave in ways you're not comfortable with? Don't tolerate their negatives; speak to them about the problems, then decide how or if they fit your world. It might be best just to let them go. Stop choosing to let them control your life, and start taking care of you.

What do all these things have in common? Your family, your friends, the media, technology, politics—they're all external. They exist outside of you. When you are externally driven, you are allowing someone or something *other than you* to control how you feel, how you act, and how successful you become in every aspect of your life—just like when you were little and you let the playground bully or some red pen marks on your homework control how you felt.

Here's the kicker—you're allowing something or someone else to decide how many cars you're going to sell this month. Right now, chances are pretty good that something else is controlling your paycheck. You'd like to take that control back—*yes*?

Internally driven people suffer, too

Now, being entirely internally driven can be just as bad for some people. Maybe you're not aware of what's going on around you. It's like you're driving along the highway of life and you just drive right on by the exits that lead to opportunities and success. You're not paying attention, and are constantly changing directions and making u-turns. You're a good person, and at some point you have to wake up and be alive. Pay attention. Participate in life. When you start to become aware of little things—like how your body feels at its best, or how you're getting along with others, or how your bank account looks—you start to become part of life. If you're reading this book, it's your time to wake up. Because you deserve it.

Some people are internally-driven, but not motivated. They don't have any reason to get up and succeed. To be motivated, you have to know what you want. Once you decide what you want, then you have to figure out if you're moving away from PROBLEMS or moving toward an amazing POSSIBILITY. Whichever it is, you have to use the PROBLEMS or POSSIBILITIES as leverage to get you up off the couch and out into the world so you can have what it is that you want. And guess what? Without knowing who you are at your best, it's tougher to get that leverage. You aren't moving in the direction of your dreams at all.

Darren Hardy, publisher of *Success Magazine*, says we all need to either find something/someone worth fighting for or find something/someone worth fighting against. Here's what I know: *You deserve to be motivated. Find your fight. Your reason. Your mission. And you'll find your motivation.*

Why is it that we don't seem to get what we want?

Has this ever happened to you? For years, you dreamed about falling in love with the right partner. The one! You know—when the hours feel like minutes? That guy or girl who makes you feel so at ease with yourself that you just can't imagine living without them. You search for that person. You hope and pray. Maybe you even visualize having this special someone in your life. And then, once he or she finally appears, BAM! You hit your Sabotage Button and it all falls to pieces. Deep down, something inside you says you might as well screw it all up quickly. There's no point in prolonging the inevitable breakup.

Why does that happen?

It happens because, on the one hand, you *want* love; but on the other hand, deep down, somewhere there's a part of you that doesn't believe you *deserve* love.

Or how about the perfect car? You want it. You dream about it. You shop for it. But as soon as it shows up, you do something to destroy it. You wreck it on the highway, or you fall behind on the payments.

Why do we do that? Why can't we be okay with our blessings?

And what about the ideal career—one that brings you wealth and happiness? You want to have lots of money. You want the mansion on the mountain with the swimming pool and movie stars for neighbors. You know you've got to make so much money for that dream to come true. And as soon as money starts showing up, what happens? Sure enough, you blow it all, you lose it all, or you make a stupid investment—and that gets rid of the money. In one hand you want wealth; in the other hand, part of you doesn't think you deserve it.

Or maybe you want respect. That's all you want. What happens as soon as you start to get respect? Chances are, you screw it up by doing something stupid. We're going to talk about respect in the next chapter. I'm going to show you exactly how people judge you on a daily basis, and how you can take control of that. For now, though, just look at the patterns in your life and realize that if you're not getting what you want, it's because at some level you don't feel worthy of having it.

It all comes down to feeling worthy of love, of wealth, of respect, of success

Worthiness is one of the reasons that people don't get what they want. The Sabotage Button shows up when what's on the outside (your desired outcome showing up) doesn't match with what's on the inside (your beliefs about your identity and what you deserve). Your mind is more powerful than external circumstances, so you unconsciously do something to get rid of the thing you want most. Then your mind sets to work rationalizing why it made you do whatever you did to sabotage yourself—you're just not lucky, you might as well screw things up quickly. You shouldn't get too high and mighty thinking you're better than everyone else.

At some point, you have to stand up and say—

I deserve it.

I'm going to get it.

It's my time.

It's my turn.

And you all need to just get out of my way!

I got this! Whatever it takes.

You are worthy just by being alive

When your sense of identity comes from the inside—when you know who you are at your best—that's when miracles happen. That's when the good stuff showing up in your life sticks around, because it matches how you see yourself on the inside. It may sound far-fetched, but once you're aware of the pattern, you'll start to see it happen all around you. Life will seem to flow; you may feel luckier and more grateful. Your awareness of your ability to achieve more will open doors that you may not have seen before. Yet they were always there.

So how do you accomplish that?

If deep down you really don't think you deserve more love, ask yourself this question: what three things does a child have to do to "deserve" his parents' love? WHAT! What kind of question is that? The child must do *nothing*. At. All. Simply by being born, children are worthy of love. They deserve food and shelter and protection from harm. It's instinct with us. We just know that when a child is born, we are supposed to love and care for it. That innocent baby doesn't have to prove she's worthy, or that she deserves to be fed. She doesn't have to "pull her weight" to deserve anything that's given to her. She just is.

At what age do we begin to build a list of items that we must have, do, or accomplish to be worthy of love? *I've got to drive this kind of car, get that grade, make this much money, live in this neighborhood, wear this type of clothes, be with this group of friends, have this body part improved, have this position in the company, get this person to like me, etc. etc. etc.* Why does a child have to do nothing, and yet we think worthiness is based on accomplishment?

You are the same person now as when you were a kid. You don't have to do anything to be *worthy* of love, a great paycheck, a happy life, or incredible relationships. You just have to accept those things, and then go do what it takes to get them. Yes, you still have to do the work. Make no mistake about that. But when you do the work, and the great money shows up—you no longer have to worry about it suddenly disappearing in a puff of smoke. Simply by accepting your worthiness, your external circumstances will match your internal identity. That symmetry helps keep the Sabotage Button from appearing.

Sabotage is tricky. It's been a part of your life for so long, you don't even know it's there. It has embedded itself into your core behavior, so that there's almost no way you can detect it unless you know to look for it.

Are you ready to rid yourself of the Sabotage Button? Let's take a look at a few ways sabotage might be controlling your everyday behavior, so you'll recognize it when you see it.

They lost my luggage

My sister is the founder of a non-profit organization called the Miracle Foundation (MiracleFoundation.org) that supports orphanages. One time I decided to go on a trek to visit her on a three-week humanitarian mission to India. The kids were magnificent! I call them the richest kids in the world. These kids have nothing—no parents, no house, no family—but they play full out. They can't wait to read you another book to show how well they're reading. They are competitive and collaborative. They'll take your leg off in a soccer game! They are ambitious and driven, and they are so happy. They love to learn and grow. They are thoughtful and kind…they are amazing. I came back from that trip completely changed!

So, I'm sitting at the baggage claim with my heart so full of all the good things I had just experienced. And just as I think the whole world is wonderful, my luggage fails to appear.

I go to the baggage claim desk and explain to them that my luggage is gone. I tell them that I have all kinds of stuff in that luggage. Good stuff—all my clothes and gifts for my mom and grandmother. I've got to get that luggage back. It's important!

They ask me if I need any clothes or anything. And I say that I'm home, and all I need is my bag back. So they tell me if they can't find my suitcase, they will give me a voucher so I can buy a new one, and replace my clothes and other items. Four weeks go by, and they still can't find my bag. So they send me the voucher to buy new stuff. Now, I had always wanted one of those high-dollar Tumi suitcases. I think, *I wouldn't buy it with my money, but I'll buy it with the airline's money!* So I went and bought the bag. And I replaced my shorts, and my t-shirts, and I got a new hat and some tennis shoes. I was still sad that all the gifts were gone, but pretty much everything in the bag was replaceable.

About a week later, I heard a knock on my door. I opened the door, and an airline courier was standing there with my luggage! He apologized for the inconvenience, and walked away. I'm thinking, *I'm so excited! My bag is back. All my stuff is back. Thank goodness it wasn't lost forever.* I opened up the suitcase and I look at my stuff and thought *oh my God.* I had been wearing some of these t-shirts and old shorts for six or seven years. I had a pair of blue jeans that might have been ten years old. They were completely worn out! I looked at my new stuff and thought *wow!* I looked so good in the new pair of jeans I just bought. I'm sorting through the suitcase, and I don't even like any of my old stuff. I'm thinking *I don't even need it.* So, I just got rid of it.

Stuck in the past?

This is one way the sabotage button can show up in your life. If this is you, your view of the world revolves around a great big rear-view mirror, and you move forward or stay in place by looking at yesterday. As soon as life shows up, and you decide to start moving in a certain direction—look out! Fear shows up. Doubt sets in. Resentment, regret, anger, sadness, or feelings of unworthiness set in, and you get paralyzed, stuck, all because something happened in your life when you were 6 or 12 or 22 or last week. You've developed this nice little fear, or sadness, or anger, or guilt to protect you from making that mistake again. Your subconscious creates fear and doubt to make sure you stay put, right where you are, and never move toward the possibility of success—because movement is risky. And if you risk, you might get hurt. You have evidence; after all, look what happened the last time. Whatever happened in the past is your excuse for not moving forward. Your brain is sneaky, too. You won't see what's happening. You'll develop addictions and habits and thought-loops to mask what's happening.

It's like you've got this big bag of worthless, disgusting garbage from the past next to your bed. And every morning you wake up and say, *"It's going to be a great day! Let me just pick up my bag of garbage from the past here."* It's really heavy, but at least it smells bad. And you walk into your job dragging your garbage with you. You go to your kid's' school dragging your garbage. You carry this bag of garbage around with you everywhere you go. You ask people, "You want to smell my garbage?" You're even willing to dump your smelly garbage with any new person who happens to come into your life.

At some point, you might want to WAKE UP! *My god, you carry this garbage from your past with you everywhere you go!* And you continually work on improving this rehearsed story that justifies your current miserable and unacceptable location in life. A location THAT YOU DON'T WANT!!!

Is it at all possible to let it go? Is it possible to say to yourself, *this is crazy. I don't want to carry this garbage around anymore?* At some point, you have to make a decision that the story—that testimony of failure you built to justify your identity of lack or scarcity—is not serving you. It's just a story you've built up over the years and embellished to make it more painful—to guarantee the probability that you'll never move past it. This fear, anger, sadness, pain, regret, hurt, resentment, and guilt you carry like a badge of honor, and it's destroying your life. It's killing your motivation. But you decide every day, *I'm going to carry this garbage with me.*

At some point, you have to wake up and say, "Enough! I'm done living the horrors of yesterday."

If you're ready to move forward and be more successful and sell more cars—you've got to get rid of your garbage. You have to get rid of the stories you've been carrying around to justify why you can't have what you want. Get rid of the fear, doubt, anger, pain—all of it. You deserve better.

I know you can let it go. (Think you'd like to let it go? To get rid of your negative past?)

You let go of stuff all the time. It's just like cleaning your closet. If you haven't worn a piece of clothing in over a year, you get rid of it. Why? Because it's no longer serving you. When you cleaned out your closet the last time, did you replace the stuff you got rid of with newer or nicer stuff? Do you even remember what you got rid of? Or is it just gone? In life, it's the same way. You get rid of stuff on a regular basis, and most of the time you don't even miss it. Just like my luggage, you don't need it anymore.

You've got to start getting rid of all that old, smelly, heavy garbage! I know you can do it. At some point in your life, you were emotionally connected to Santa Claus, the Easter Bunny, the Tooth Fairy, and Hannukah Harry, and you managed to give them away. You can give up your other stories, too. You let Santa go, but you're still holding onto the story of a teacher who embarrassed you or a kid who called you a name 25 years ago. Why? At some point, you have to decide *this is lunacy! It's gone as of right now!* When you do that and move on from the past and focus on who you are at your best, you have a better chance of embracing NOW.

Stuck in the future?

All the way in the future. I'm talking about that $460 million dollar lottery ticket you buy every week. (Nod your head if this is you.) Some folks are so stuck in the future that when they buy that ticket, they go into a hazy dream world—totally gone from reality! Don't get me wrong, looking into the future and seeing the possibilities is great. But staying in the future all the time is a problem. Going to bed at night dreaming about what you can do with money you've never had is lunacy! You've got to pick the future you want, and then get back to the present. Get back to where your gold mine is, and start shoveling. It takes focus and work.

You don't live in yesterday, and you can't live in tomorrow. What you do have is NOW. The present is the best gift you've got—for yourself, for your customers, and for your kids and loved ones.

Be present—Be who you are at your best

I'm right here. I'm present. I'm paying attention to the words I'm typing and saying to you. I'm present in life right now. I care about you. I respect you. I don't even know you, but I know that you deserve that care and respect just because you're alive.

At some point you have to say, *I'm here. Right here. And here is perfect.* When you're in the present moment, you're in charge of everything, and life is amazing. You've probably been searching for who you are in the past and in the future. But where you'll find out who you truly are is in the present.

When you're present in a sales conversation, you can see yourself being kind, helpful, resourceful, and fun. When you're present talking to your neighbor about how her husband just had a wreck and she's worried that they'll get ripped off when they go to get a new vehicle, you can be present and see how to best help your neighbor. Guys, put down the TV clicker; you are not present when you're watching your favorite show. You're only half doing two jobs. Your spouse thinks you are ignoring her, and you hate her, and you're not happy with her, and you want a divorce, and she doesn't look good, and you're sleeping with the imaginary girlfriend!! Stop. Push mute or off, turn towards her, smile, nod your head "yes," and listen. Keep your mouth shut and listen. You can thank me later; she'll thank you immediately.

Managers, when your phone is ringing on your desk and you have no idea who it is, that unknown person IS NOT more important to you than the salesperson working a deal with you at that moment. Be present with your employees. The greatest leaders I know in this business give people their full attention and presence.

Opportunities are all around you. Money is everywhere if you just stay present long enough to become aware of it. When you sleepwalk through your life, or live in the past, you miss so much! When you spend your whole day dreaming about the future, you don't see the doors opening up in front of you—the very doors that could take you to that future you're dreaming about.

Be present. Wake up. Pay attention. And be who you are at your best. Suddenly, the whole world will open up at your feet, and you'll wonder why you ever thought it was so difficult.

Who you really are at your best

The I AM chart in this section (fig 3.2) shows about 130 different qualities, characteristics, and values. About 70 percent of them are you. What I want you to do right now is take the time to go through each one and write "I am" in front of the ones that describe you at your best. Do not put a checkmark or a squiggly line. "I AM" is your connection to your greatness. It is your connection to your source of godliness when you're positively labeling yourself. This is for you. This is about you. Do it! And as you're doing it, pay special attention to the words that are *definitely you*. As you read through the list, some of the characteristics and values will scream I REALLY AM this! Circle these words, or put an asterisk next to them. They speak to you at your deepest level.

On my list, I have: *I am lucky* (I'm the luckiest person you've ever met in your life). I am happy. I am fun. I am peaceful. I am quirky. I am kind. I am giving. I am intuitive. I am loving. I am inspirational. I am creative. I am simple. These words are truly me, and they define my brilliance on a regular basis. Also on this list are the characteristics, values, and traits that I suck at. Pay attention to these as well. You're going to want to learn how to avoid these in your life. I AM very unorganized. There was a time in my life where I thought, *if only I was organized, then I'd be successful.* I later discovered that if I worked really, really, really hard at organization, the best I could achieve is average—and miserable. No one pays you massive amounts of money to achieve average. Figure out what you are good at and become great. Be aware of what you suck at, avoid it, and find a way to accomplish it more easily.

Please take the time to do this right now. It's important. And as you're going through this list, building your identity from the inside, I want you to think about how *amazing* this person is—how thoughtful, clever, and articulate, and whatever else you put down. Take the time to appreciate yourself.

Do this on this page. Okay, go!

I AM Adventurous	___ Emotional	___ Inspirational	___ Quick Witted
I AM Articulate	___ Extraordinary	___ Imaginative	___ Responsible
I AM Agreeable	___ Easy going	___ Industrious	___ Remarkable
I AM Alive	___ Empathetic	___ IMPRESSIVE	___ Reliable
I AM Appreciative	___ Excited	___ Joyful	___ Rich
I AM Accepting	___ Explicit	___ Kind	___ Resourceful
I AM Attractive	___ Entertaining	___ Knowledgeable	___ Strong
___ Attentive	___ Fearless	___ Lucky	___ Selfless
___ Artistic	___ Flexible	___ Logical	___ Self Assured
___ Athletic	___ Friendly	___ Loyal	___ Social
___ Attentive	___ Faithful	___ Loved	___ Simple
___ Authentic	___ Fashionable	___ Loving	___ Self-Aware
___ Blessed	___ Forgiving	___ Magnetic	___ Smart
___ Bubbly	___ Frugal	___ Musical	___ Self-Sufficient
___ Brave	___ Funny	___ Mechanical	___ Sincere
___ Bright	___ Giving	___ Memorable	___ Thoughtful
___ Bold	___ Giggly	___ Motivated	___ Technical
___ Brilliant	___ Godly	___ Neat	___ Thankful
___ Calm	___ Grateful	___ Noble	___ Teachable
___ Charismatic	___ Gentle	___ Organized	___ Truthful
___ Crafty	___ Geeky	___ Outstanding	___ Thorough
___ Creative	___ Generous	___ Open	___ Tenacious
___ Clear	___ Happy	___ Optimistic	___ Thrifty
___ Compelling	___ Helpful	___ Playful	___ Up Beat
___ Considerate	___ Honorable	___ Present	___ Understanding
___ Caring	___ Honest	___ Passionate	___ Unstoppable
___ Dynamic	___ Harmonious	___ Polite	___ Unique
___ Driven	___ Healthy	___ Peaceful	___ Versatile
___ Disciplined	___ Handsome	___ Pretty	___ Visionary
___ Different	___ Independent	___ Powerful	___ Vulnerable
___ Detailed	___ Inventive	___ Persistent	___ Willing
___ Determined	___ Intuitive	___ Quick	___ Wise
___ Energetic	___ Influential	___ Quiet	___ YES Driven

Who is this person you just described?
Is this person worthy of love?

Is this person worthy of respect?

Is this person worthy of success and wealth?

Does this person deserve great relationships with friends and family?

Does this person deserve an unstoppable, proud, bold, profitable, happy life?

Does this person *believe* what they desire is possible?

At some point in all our lives, we come to the conclusion that in order to be worthy, we have to possess the external icons of success. We have to drive a nice car, or live in a nice house, or make a lot of money, or buy her nice things, or take him to fancy restaurants. And when that relationship falls apart, we think *but I'm doing all these things to be worthy, why isn't it working?*

The answer is: *you are seeking external validation, when the truth is inside you.* You aren't deserving because of external things; you are deserving simply because of who you are on the inside. That's it.

Look at your list again. Is that person worthy of love? Of course he is! Does that person deserve success? Absolutely she does!

This is natural behavior. It's how we were born to BE.

Your self-doubts, fears, and feelings of unworthiness go out the window when you just BE yourself at your best. Because who you are is godly. You are perfect at your best.

If I had asked you to write down 20 things you're bad at, most people would have no trouble at all. Because the media and society tell us all the time where we are lacking. In our society, our parents told us everything we didn't do well. In our society, we were graded on a report card, and we only looked at the bad marks. It didn't matter if we worked our butts off to get "B" grades, the ones that stood out were the Ds or Fs. Because for generations, that's how we were taught to judge ourselves—by looking at life through other people's labels and our shortcomings. But that's not who we are—or who you are.

This list is the *real you*. Now you know.

When you judge yourself based on your internal reflection, rather than on how you think society sees you, or how your teachers saw you, or your parents, or the playground bully, or your boss—then life is sweet. Start seeing yourself and living your life by who you really are.

How do you use your list to get what you want?

Now that you know who you are, and that nothing is going to hold that person back, you have to find a way to use the list you created to bring *that person* to life. How can you make it so that who you are at your best is how you behave every day? How do you manifest that person into being every day? You do it by paying attention to the areas of your life that make you alive. You use your list as leverage to get what you want in your profession, your health, your relationships, and your personal growth. Any aspect of your life that you want to grow, you can do it using your list. Since this is a book about sales, let's focus on your profession. If you are selling cars, how can you use who you are at your best to sell more cars and build the career of your dreams? What do you do every day to be who you are at your best?

To be happy and successful in your profession, you've got to be proud of what you do. And most people gain more pride by doing something for someone else than by doing something for themselves. You need to have a bigger reason for doing what you do than just selling a car, or a boat, or a motorcycle. That bigger reason is your mission, and it's the key to escaping your job and having a great profession you're proud of (and making massive amounts of money while you're at it).

Having a mission is how those top sellers in your dealership make it look so easy. I used to look at those guys and think, *Wow. They're selling 30 cars, and I'm struggling to sell 10. They make it look so simple. How do they do that? They're no better than me; what's going on?* You see, they found a way to make it work. They found a way to bring their profession to life. And by the end of this book, you'll know the secret to making it work, too. (You're already off to a great start.)

Who you are is not what you do.
You are a human being, not a human *doing*.

WHO "I AM" and where am I Going

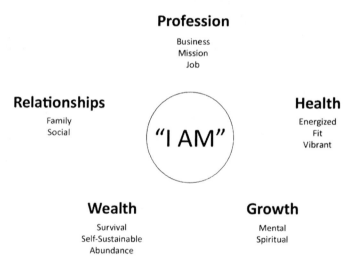

Profession
Business
Mission
Job

Relationships
Family
Social

"I AM"

Health
Energized
Fit
Vibrant

Wealth
Survival
Self-Sustainable
Abundance

Growth
Mental
Spiritual

Who you are at your best applies to all areas of your life.

What you do is not who you are. It's how you feed your family, and provide resources, and have a mission-driven life that has purpose. But you're much more than that. In order to be who you are at your best and have the life of your dreams, you have to pay attention to a few things besides work.

Fit and Healthy. Did you know that the average person in the United States dies in their late 70's? How many retired salespeople do you know that age? How many retired managers do you know that age? Where are they? I recently was told a shocking statistic that the average person in the car business dies in their early 60's! If this statistic is true, then you have to ask, "What's up with that?" How is it that we die 10 years or more sooner than the average person?

Well, for starters, have you ever paid attention to how salespeople and managers eat in the car industry? Maybe you go all day without eating because, after all, you're working and that's more important. When you finally do realize you're hungry, you go up to the conference room and slam down four pieces of leftover pizza and a Coke in less than four minutes. Or you find it okay to eat your hamburger cold and your soft drink warm—all so you can rush back downstairs to find the next customer. That is not healthy. Really. Pay attention to how people around you eat in this business, and you will be amazed. We treat our bodies terribly, and then try to fix all the problems with coffee and 5-hour energy and Red Bull and medicine and chemicals. I have a dear friend in this business who recently had bypass surgery. He said it was the most painful thing he'd ever experienced. He wouldn't wish it on his worst enemy. The man is only 46 years old!

There's no need for it. You deserve a fit, healthy, vibrant body. You deserve to be energetic all the time. And you can have that, but you have to wake up and pay attention. Look at your list. What qualities, characteristics, and values do you need every day to be vibrant and healthy?

I am energetic.
I am happy.
I am vibrant.
I am unstoppable.
What else?

I AM *energetic*   I AM _____

I AM *happy*   I AM _____

I AM *vibrant*   I AM _____

I AM *unstoppable*   I AM _____

I AM _____   I AM _____

I AM _____   I AM _____

I AM _____   I AM _____

I AM _____   I AM _____

I AM _____   I AM _____

I AM _____   I AM _____

I AM _____   I AM _____

I AM _____   I AM _____

I AM _____   I AM _____

I AM _____   I AM _____

I AM _____   I AM _____

I AM _____   I AM _____

I AM _____   I AM _____

I AM _____   I AM _____

I AM _____   I AM _____

I AM _____   I AM _____

I AM _____   I AM _____

I AM _____   I AM _____

I AM _____   I AM _____

I AM _____   I AM _____

I AM _____   I AM _____

I AM _____   I AM _____

I AM _____   I AM _____

I AM _____   I AM _____

Relationships. How do you treat the people closest to you—your family, your spouse, your children, your friends—and how do they treat you? So often, we are completely engrossed in work and have no idea what's happening to the people we love the most. We ignore everyone until something bad happens, and we're forced to pay attention. Our children get into trouble at school because that's the only way they can get us to pay attention to them. We have to wake up and nurture the good relationships in our lives.

Equally important is how people treat you. Some of you may need to get rid of the energy-sucking vampire relationships that drain you of your will to live. If you have people in your life who just suck—get rid of them! You don't need them. Spend your precious energy on the people who matter—the people you love. You deserve strong and rewarding relationships. What qualities, characteristics, and values do you need every day to have awesome relationships?

I am present.
I am loving.
I am generous.
I am happy.
What else?

I AM *present*	I AM _____
I AM *happy*	I AM _____
I AM *loving*	I AM _____
I AM *generous*	I AM _____
I AM _____	I AM _____
I AM _____	I AM _____
I AM _____	I AM _____
I AM _____	I AM _____

I AM _____   I AM _____
I AM _____   I AM _____
I AM _____   I AM _____
I AM _____   I AM _____
I AM _____   I AM _____
I AM _____   I AM _____
I AM _____   I AM _____
I AM _____   I AM _____
I AM _____   I AM _____
I AM _____   I AM _____
I AM _____   I AM _____
I AM _____   I AM _____
I AM _____   I AM _____
I AM _____   I AM _____
I AM _____   I AM _____
I AM _____   I AM _____
I AM _____   I AM _____
I AM _____   I AM _____
I AM _____   I AM _____
I AM _____   I AM _____
I AM _____   I AM _____
I AM _____   I AM _____
I AM _____   I AM _____

Growth. When you want your life to improve, you want growth. Newness is good. It means you're improving in life. Staying stagnant and stuck in one place is not an option for you. You prefer to learn new things and apply them in your life. That could mean spiritual growth or mental growth. For spiritual growth, what are you doing to build a spiritual connection with whatever or whoever you believe is the source of your better self?

For the mental side, what are you filling your head with? What are you reading? Is it worth paying attention to? Your brain has the ability to grow and improve. Paying attention to your growth means taking responsibility for your own education, too. It means figuring things out and making them work for you. Formal education in school and college is great, but you're not going to truly grow and get what you want until you self-educate. You have to find out how the world works. What makes people do what they do, and how can you put that knowledge to your own advantage? Never let a formal education get in the way of your magnificence and your gifts.

You deserve to grow and learn and get smart about life so you can get whatever you want.

What qualities, characteristics, and values do you need every day to grow and expand in life?

I am curious.

I am inquisitive.

I am adventurous.

I am fearless.

What else?

I AM *curious*	I AM _____
I AM *inquisitive*	I AM _____
I AM *adventurous*	I AM _____
I AM *fearless*	I AM _____
I AM _____	I AM _____
I AM _____	I AM _____
I AM _____	I AM _____

I AM _____	I AM _____
I AM _____	I AM _____
I AM _____	I AM _____
I AM _____	I AM _____
I AM _____	I AM _____
I AM _____	I AM _____
I AM _____	I AM _____
I AM _____	I AM _____
I AM _____	I AM _____
I AM _____	I AM _____
I AM _____	I AM _____
I AM _____	I AM _____
I AM _____	I AM _____
I AM _____	I AM _____
I AM _____	I AM _____
I AM _____	I AM _____
I AM _____	I AM _____
I AM _____	I AM _____
I AM _____	I AM _____
I AM _____	I AM _____
I AM _____	I AM _____
I AM _____	I AM _____
I AM _____	I AM _____
I AM _____	I AM _____

Wealth. Think about the abundance of valuable material possessions—property, money, and resources. When I first got a job in the auto industry, I was definitely not wealthy. Quite the opposite. I was like most people who get into our business, broke and in survival mode. I was late on my rent with no money coming in and struggling.

I wanted out of the struggle. I wanted to pay my bills easily and on time for a change. I wanted to move away from survival mode to being self-sustainable. You've heard me call this business opportunity a gold mine. It truly is a vehicle to accomplish your greatest dreams. In this business, you definitely have the ability to move from self-sustainability to abundance—and wealth beyond your current dreams. Remember all the stories of people moving from struggle to success? This is what's possible for you.

Making the money is simple. You can collect $2 million in twenty years with just a little improvement each year. Let me prove it to you.

Make only $3,000 a month the first year, then just improve 10 percent.

You're making $3,300 a month in year two, improve another 10 percent.

You're making $4,200 a month in year three, improve another10 percent.

$4,620 the next year.	=	$55,440 per year
$5,082 the next.	=	$60,984 per year
$5,590 the next.	=	$67,080 per year

Is it possible to increase your business by 10 percent? By 20 percent? Over 20 years, you will earn $2 million. Do the math. It's amazing. That's a lot of money. Your life and your business are yours.

Your raise becomes effective when you do—not when your management does, or the advertising does, or the economy does. You must build yourself and be better. You deserve it. What qualities, characteristics, and values do you need every day to be truly abundant?

I am consistent.

I am knowledgeable.

I am flexible.
I am frugal.
What else?

I AM *consistent*

I AM *frugal*

I AM *knowledgeable*

I AM *flexible*

I AM _____

I AM _____

I AM _____

I AM _____

I AM _____

I AM _____

I AM _____

I AM _____

I AM _____

I AM _____

I AM _____

I AM _____

I AM _____

I AM _____

I AM _____

I AM _____

I AM _____

I AM _____

I AM _____

I AM _____

I AM _____

I AM _____

I AM _____

I AM _____

I AM _____

I AM _____

I AM _____

I AM _____

I AM _____

I AM _____

I AM _____

I AM _____

I AM _____

I AM _____

I AM _____

I AM _____

I AM _____

I AM _____

If all you want to do is sell more cars, take a step back. Examine these other areas. You deserve to have a fit, vibrant, healthy body. You deserve to have relationships with family and friends that lift you up and make life wonderful. You deserve to grow and expand your life in any way you desire. And you are worthy of wealth—true abundance—not just sustainability.

You will have all those things. And I'm going to show you how to get them.

Applying your list to your whole life

Here's a little secret. You have to be willing to fail. I mean fail big! I want you to set a destination in your mind that is so huge and so far away you just think, *Holy crap, there is NO WAY I can make that happen. Never in a million years!* And then I want you to set off for it. I want you to fail big. I want you to fail hard, fail often, and I want you to fail fast. Don't drag it out; go full blast. Yes, occasionally you're going to screw up and succeed. You'll just have to live with that.

Most people are so afraid to set out and fail that they never set out and win. They never set out at all. They stay stuck where they are in survival mode, and that's no way to live. I want you to look at each of the five areas of your life (profession, health, relationships, growth, and wealth) and set a destination.

Set a course.

Find a direction.

Build a mission that says, *It's my time. I deserve to get what I want. And that means I'm going to have THAT house, and THAT car, and THAT amazing relationship with my spouse, THAT amazing life.*

And when people say, "Man, what planet are you living on?"

You just answer, "The one I'm building."

You're building your own reality, your own planet. The one you want to live on. With the friends that fill your soul and make you happy. With a fit, healthy, and energetic body. Build your world the way you want it. Dream big. Insanely big! Or insanely simple. Whatever you want—it's possible.

Then take a look at your list, at who you are at your best, and decide how *that* person is going to live his or her life. Because *that* *person* isn't going to let anything stand in the way. And that person is *you*. You get to decide which qualities you're going to adopt today. If you want something, look at your list and ask yourself, *what qualities, characteristics, and values do I already have that will create the outcome I want?* Then embody those characteristics throughout the day. It's easy. It's natural. This is already who you are. You don't have to try, just be.

This is why it's so important for you to have your list handy. And if for some crazy reason you decided to skip those exercises, go back and do them now. You'll be grateful you did. Do the work of getting good at being you.

Build your dream world by doing
your job better than anybody else

I interviewed a wonderful older gentleman recently. A few years ago, his family found out that he was an incredible war hero. He had a box full of medals that they never knew about. In nine months of serving in Korea, this man somehow managed to win the Silver Star and two Bronze Stars (one with a combat "V" for valor under fire). He was nominated for the Congressional Medal of Honor, and if he'd been dead, he'd have gotten it. He had a letter of commendation that said he was above and beyond, *crazy* good at doing what he did in Korea. In addition to all this, he had a purple heart for an injury he sustained in the field when doctors had to piece his leg back together. Now, the purple heart—that was his medal. He was proud of that medal. The others were all stuffed in a box in the back of a closet.

When the family finally asked him about the medals, all he said was, "*That's all bullshit.*"

They pressed on and told him, "No—these medals are a huge deal. What in the world happened?"

He said, "I don't want to talk about that. This one here, the Purple Heart, this is the one I earned."

"But what about all these other medals?"

"I didn't earn those. All I was doing was my job. They told me my job was to go get that Marine—the one lying on the ground screaming in pain—patch him up, and get him safely to the hospital. That's what they said my job was. Get the Marine. Bring him back to the hospital. I'm a corpsman, that's what I did. They didn't say, '*Only do your job if there's only one Marine hurt.*' They didn't say, '*Only get the Marine if it isn't snowing.*' They didn't say, '*Only get the Marine if your leg isn't injured.*' They said, '*Do Your Damn Job!*' My job was to help those Marines and get them back to the hospital. And If I did it fast enough, those boys had a chance to live their lives. And that's what I did. I just did my job. I didn't do anything heroic."

That's how successful people think. Do YOUR job. That's how you create the world you want. Just do your job. So many people come into a business to get a job, and the first thing they do is decide they want someone else's job. They are so ambitious and want to get ahead so badly, that they never do their own jobs. They have all the best intentions, but they just don't see that the best way to be successful in life is to be simple. Whatever your job is, find out what it's about. And do that job better than anybody else—to the best of your ability.

Your job is selling cars. So, find out everything you need to know about selling cars, and go do it better than anyone else. You'll succeed. I guarantee it.

Use your list to find out what qualities, characteristics, and values you need to do your job better

This is it, right here. This is how you make success happen. Look at your list, and figure out which of the many characteristics you wrote down will help you do whatever you need to do that day.

Step 1: Ask yourself, what characteristics do I need to do my job today? Then write them down.

I am committed.
I am entertaining.
I am interesting.
I am thoughtful.
I am heartfelt.
I am bold.
I am charismatic.
I am influential.
I am resourceful.
I am flexible.
I am articulate.
I am intuitive.
I am lucky.

Write down everything you are that will help you do your job better. Then you'll want to take that big list and narrow it down to ten or so things that you need right now. It's like a recipe for success.

Step 2: Take that list that you wrote and narrow it down even more. Write down three to five characteristics of who you are at your best in your job. What do you need most right now?

Step 3. Then take those three to five words and write a mission statement. When I was selling cars, my mission statement was—*I am interesting, entertaining, and fun so that I can help people get cars.* Now my mission is—*To influence, educate, and inspire you to love and believe in yourself, so that you can have the life you deserve with everything you want—happiness, health, an incredible bank account, with family and friends around you, and knowledge that just drips over your brain—that's what you deserve.*

Here's the easiest way I've found to write a mission statement. Just fill in the first three blanks below with words from your I AM list. Then fill in the end of the sentence with the result you want to help people achieve.

Primary Mission Statement

What qualities, characteristics, and values must I have so that I am successful, productive, and proud of my profession?

Your profession is a great place to start with building a mission statement. After you complete that, you can focus on the other areas in your life. Who are you at your best with your health, your relationships, your growth, and your wealth? Go through the same steps and create mission statements for those areas, too.

Fit and Healthy Mission Statement

What qualities, characteristics, and values must I have so that I can have a fit, health, energetic, and happy body? Write your list and then narrow it down to what will drive you.

I am _____   I am _____

I am _____   I am _____

I am _____   I am _____

I am _____   I am _____

I am _____   I am _____

I am _____   I am _____

I am _____   I am _____

I am _____   I am _____

I am _____, _____, and _____ so that

_____.

Relationship Mission Statement:
Personal, Professional, and Social

What qualities, characteristics, and values must I have so that I can have lifelong meaningful and fulfilling relationships? Write your list and then narrow it down to what will drive you.

I am _____   I am _____

I am _____   I am _____

I am _____   I am _____

I am _____   I am _____

I am _____   I am _____

I am _____   I am _____

I am _____   I am _____

I am _____   I am _____

I am _____, _____, and _____ so that

_____.

Growth Mission Statement: Mental and Spiritual

What qualities, characteristics, and values must I have so that I can discover, learn, and grow? Write your list and then narrow it down to what will drive you.

I am _____   I am _____

I am _____   I am _____

I am _____   I am _____

I am _____   I am _____

I am _____   I am _____

I am _____   I am _____

I am _____, _____, and _____ so that _____.

Wealth Mission Statement

What qualities, characteristics and values must I have so that I can be wealthy? Write your list and then narrow it down to what will drive you.

I am _____   I am _____

I am _____   I am _____

I am _____   I am _____

I am _____   I am _____

I am _____   I am _____

I am _____   I am _____

I am _____, _____, and _____ so that _____.

Go ahead. Take the time to fill these out. Pull the words directly from your list of qualities, characteristics, and values. Those words are you at your best. They come from inside you. So use them here to build your mission.

So what's possible for you?

Can you live fuller? Play bigger? Do you deserve success, happiness, wealth, love, respect, and success?

DO IT NOW! Do the work.

Simply because you're reading this book, I believe it is your time. I also know this: if you don't take action and do this work, it's not going to happen as fast as you deserve. You want it now. Do your job now. Take the time to imagine what it will be like. When you are who you are at your best, and if you live that every day, what's possible in your life? Where do you live? Who do you have around you? How's your health? How's your relationship with your children or your significant other?

This is the foundation for selling more cars and building the life of your dreams. Take the time to do the exercises in this chapter, and I promise you that your life will improve for the better. It has to. It can't help but get better, because you will be living who you are at your best every day.

If you haven't already, do the exercises now.

Own it!

It's time for you to implement what you've learned so far.

I know you've already written down all the exercises in the book here. But I've also created some downloadable sheets that you can print and post where you'll see them. Maybe you keep your list on your bedside table to remind you of who you are at your best. Maybe you stash your mission statements in your desk at work, or in your wallet. Sooner or later, you're going to have all this just showing up every day. It will be a part of you, and you won't have to think about it. But at first, you're probably going to need to see your list now and then to remind you.

So, go to http://AutoTrainingAcademy.com/mission-statement/ and download those sheets and print them off. You'll be glad you did.

BREAK THE RULES...WRITE IN THE BOOK!

_____
_____
_____
_____
_____
_____
_____
_____
_____
_____
_____
_____
_____
_____
_____
_____
_____
_____
_____
_____
_____
_____
_____
_____
_____

Chapter Four

HOW ARE YOU JUDGED?

"Live by the Rules of Engagement."

I n order to "get good at you" and "serve others," you have to understand how human beings tend to judge each other. I'm not just talking about individuals here. I'm talking about how your company is judged. How your children are judged. How your culture is judged by others.

I recently had an experience in a local business where I was treated horribly. Really, really bad. And I wasn't the only one treated this way. I left that establishment with the commitment that I would never go there again. Now in the old days, I might have told five or six people about my experience, and that would be the end of it. But not anymore. I told 1,500 people on my Facebook page. I posted a bad review on Yelp. I made sure everybody knew that this company sucked!

Let me tell you, my email and my Facebook page blew up. I had messages coming at me from every perspective with a few saying that I was over generalizing. I was judging a whole company based on one bad employee. And my little sister, who I adore, sent me a text that said, "*You cannot judge that whole company based on one bad employee. I have good friends who work there. They are good people. You cannot say those kinds of things.*" I immediately recognized the harm I had done. So, I went back to Facebook, and I apologized. I said I knew it was wrong to judge the whole place by one person, and I wouldn't do it again. As a matter of fact, I said I would go back and do business with them again.

So, I went back a few times, and sure enough, I was treated terribly again. I was shocked and angry at myself. I knew better. I came back because of this company's "good people," but I was wrong. I learned then that I should judge your company based on your sorriest employee. When I complain to management, nothing is done. Nothing changes. So, your company's *worst* employee is how I will evaluate your whole business from now on. If you're the owner of a company, your greatest horror is for people to say that *you* treat people badly—possibly because of just *one* of your employees.

Think about this. When you apply for a job, you have to fill out an application. On that application, you have to tell them you had a DUI, or some other negative event, more than 30 years ago. The company is surely going to ask if you've rehabilitated yourself from that behavior. They're going to make sure that they protect themselves *from you*, because of what you did way back when. Make no mistake about it. You are being judged by your worst day on this planet. Similarly, your company is being judged by its worst employee. If you're the business owner, you probably don't even know how much that employee is costing you because not everyone complains. But when they do complain, what's done about it? That's the question.

People do this to you all the time. They judge you by your worst day, or by your worst employee. One little mistake will haunt you for your whole entire life, because that's how people judge you. In life, every time you treat someone unkindly, they leave. And they decide never to come back. These days, one bad review can destroy an entire company. One employee having a bad day can seriously impact a business.

I went out to eat a while back, and I ordered a taco salad. I was so excited to have a taco salad that afternoon. But I always have trouble deciding what dressing to order. So I asked the waiter what he recommended as a dressing. He said he didn't really know because he didn't eat taco salads, but sour cream might be good. So, I decided to try it. He brought out one little dollop of sour cream, and it wasn't enough. So, I asked him to get another little dollop. I mixed it all up and it was delicious! I couldn't wait to give the waiter a good tip because I had such a wonderful experience. And then I got the bill. I was charged $1.30 a piece for my two dollops of dressing. I didn't know that they would charge me to add sour cream; I just thought I was using it as a salad dressing. So, I told the waiter.

He looked at me, rolled his eyes, and then said, "Sir, we don't just give sour cream without charging you." Obviously, I was the only one who didn't understand this worldwide sour cream policy. I paid the bill, and I tipped him one dollar because I really felt like he blew it.

As I was leaving, the manager asked how I enjoyed my meal. I didn't want to make a big deal out of it; so I just casually mentioned to her what happened so she would know to tell the next customer about the extra charge. I thought that would be the end of it. I just wouldn't come back to that restaurant, and life would go on.

But she said, "Oh, let me take care of that." She took my receipt, and I thought she was going to give me my $2.60 back. But she didn't. She picked up the tab on our whole ticket—two lunches.

I said, "No, that's not necessary. We enjoyed our meals, and we want to pay for them." But she insisted. She said we were not going to pay for our meals, and in addition, she gave us a pre-paid $25 gift card just so we could come back again. Because she knew if we came back, we were going to love how they did business.

Well I did go back. And I do love the way they do business. And I've told everybody I know about this great little Mexican place called Casa Mañana in Lake Charles, Louisiana. And I'm going to keep telling people. I love that place!

What does this have to do with selling cars?

Remember, the business of your business is people, and the key to massive success is building and maintaining lifelong relationships. So, if people are judging you every day, the same people who might buy a car from you, or who might know someone who might buy a car from you—don't you think it's wise to treat people like royalty all the time? Imagine what this world would be like if everybody treated everybody else like royalty. The world would be amazing! It's not likely to happen anytime soon. But wouldn't it be nice?

Remember what you learned in the last chapter about building your own planet? You learned that you can build your world any way you want. That goes for how people are treated, as well. You get to decide how people perceive you, and how they judge you. When you set up your world so that people judge you to be kind and honest and trustworthy, do you think you're going to sell more cars? You better believe it!

So how do you navigate your life so that even on your worst day people still think you're awesome? How do you make sure people are judging you the way you want to be judged?

Rules of Engagement

The way you do this is to have rules of engagement—a set of standards or values that you do not deviate from. Ever. Even if others around you behave differently, even if they call you crazy, you stick to your standards. Remember, this is *your* business. This is *your* planet. You are the boss of you—or at least, you are the boss of how you behave. If you follow these three rules, you won't go wrong.

Rule #1: Customers First

The first rule of engagement in your business is to make *everything* customer driven. Everything must work for the customer. Go back to your "I AM" list. How does that person treat everybody he comes in contact with? Does that person treat people like royalty? Does that person help the customer get what she wants? That person is you. The customer has to come first. And remember, the customer could be *anyone* you come in contact with. We're going to talk about that more when we get into building relationships. For now, just realize that you never know who the customer is. It could be anyone. So, your first rule of engagement is that you always treat other people like royalty, no matter who they are.

In the car business, some talk badly about our customers because they have bad credit, or they don't have any money, or they drive ugly cars, or whatever. Sometimes we treat people badly because they talk funny or look funny.

Enough! Stop negatively labeling other human beings. Everyone has value. This business is a goldmine, if we can just love and care for our customers better. You can treat them like royalty, no matter what their credit score is. I know you want to. Would our industry be better if we treated customers and employees better? Does the person on your list appreciate other people? Of course. And the reason is because you appreciate yourself. If you appreciate yourself, then you can appreciate everybody. That's what this business is all about. You need to take better care of people. You need to be dialed in to lifelong relationships—not just one-night stands. It's about saying, "I've got you. I'm going to take care of you forever."

That's the first rule—customer first. Become an advocate. Whatever it takes.

Rule #2: Employee Driven

You are the employee in your business. Whatever is going on around you, it has to work for you. For me personally, everything has to come from my heart. I'm an emotional and passionate person. If my business is all up in my head, then I'm not comfortable dealing with other people. I need what I do to be in integrity with who I am at my best. You might be different. You might need to make this business work a little differently. Maybe you need flexible hours because your family needs you to be there for them at certain times. Maybe you need permission to ignore the sales scripts and come up with your own way of talking to people. Whatever you need to do to make this business work for you is okay, as long as it meets Rule #1 first. Then if it works for the customer, and it works for you, the only other guideline you need is to be completely honest.

Rule #3: 100 Percent Honesty

You need to be 100 percent in integrity all the time. There is no such thing as an inconsequential lie. All lies are painful. All lies have consequences. In our industry, some lies are taught to get people in the door—*Come on down, we've got it in stock.* (When you don't.) While other lies are tolerated to sell an insurance product that the bank requires, when they don't.

The lies I used to tell made me look like an idiot to my customers. Managers said the less I knew, the better off I was. You know what? That's not true. The truth is that people who sell lots of cars know it all; and the overwhelming majority tell the truth so that it works for them and for the customer. They follow the three rules of engagement. They take better care of people, and they sell more cars.

Customer—Employee—Honesty.

Treat People Like Royalty; It's that simple.

Okay, now that we're all on the same page with how to treat people so they judge us in a positive light, let's kick it up a notch. Let's talk about customer expectations. After all, if you don't know what they expect, how can you make sure everything works for them?

What do customers expect?

Customers want to feel special. They have a lot of expectations, and this is the biggest one. They want to feel like the most important person in your world at that moment. One way you make them feel that way is to just be present. I mean 100 percent present there with them, paying attention to what they say, paying attention to their body language. Be present in that moment. Be dialed in to those customers and really listen to them. Respect who they are. If you do that, they're going to feel like they connect with you. They're going to trust you. It's going to be like they've known you their whole lives.

There will be people who walk into your store and do not want to like you, or trust you, or even be around you. They'll say, "LEAVE ME ALONE." Three hours later, they're buying a new car from you. They're handing over $2,000 to the F&I department and saying, "You know, we didn't even come in to buy a car today." Have you ever had this happen to you? Do you think that's normal? Why is it that a customer can come on the lot and want nothing to do with you, and two hours later, he's trusting you with enough information to commit identity theft? The customer trusts you because you're present, and you respect them. That makes them feel special, and we all like to feel special. This is how you want to treat everyone in your life, not just potential customers. Everyone you talk to should feel that way. Isn't that what you want for yourself? To like others and be liked by others?

Customers want more value than price. They don't want "cheap". They want a vehicle that solves their Problems or moves them toward new Possibilities. They want to know the car fits them perfectly. Later on when we discuss the Keep it Simple Selling process, I'm going to show you exactly how to ask the right questions and Get The Picture of what "more value" means to that customer. It's different every time. Every customer wants to move away from their Problems and toward a better Possibility. So, I'm going to show you how to figure out what that better Possibility is for each and every person you talk to. For now, just realize this is one of the most important customer expectations. They don't want "cheap"; they want value. By giving them more value than price, they will feel they got the perfect car from the right person.

Do whatever it takes. That's it. Just do whatever it takes. No less. If you do whatever it takes to help customers—if you just do your job better than everyone else—you will wind up with more sales. There is no competition.

Welcome to the dealership. Acknowledge everyone who walks in. Smile, be present, and listen to them. It's not that difficult to meet this expectation; just say, "Hi! Welcome to the dealership. Thanks for coming in today." They want to be welcomed by everyone, not just the one person who might benefit from their business. Pay attention, wake up, be aware.

Customers want exceptional service. They want the best. Good service isn't good enough. They want to know that the service they got was above and beyond what they expected. Make sure people leave your company saying, "WOW!"

Do it NOW. They don't want to wait. Deliver what they want immediately. Let them know how much time you are going to take, and keep them updated on the progress. No excuses, be considerate of their time.

Deliver WOW. You deliver that moment, and they're hooked. Most people are just trying to get *through* their customer and on to the next one. Don't be most people. Get your customers to experience *WOW,* and you will see a rise in your paycheck. You can't wow people doing someone else's job. Just DO YOUR JOB—better than anyone else. Be present. Over deliver.

Always be honest. My mother used to tell us, "Before you say anything, ask yourself three questions: *is what I'm about to say true, is it kind, and is it necessary?*" Lying does not serve you. Here's the thing— most of the time when you tell an untrue story, it's at the beginning of a relationship when you're trying to look more impressive than you think you are. So you lie to gain the other person's trust or admiration. This is not necessary, because the customers want you to be focused on them and their needs, not how important you look. Another time you lie is when you try to give the impression that you know it all. Again, this is unnecessary because the customer cares about how much you care about them, not how much you know about everything. Stop embellishing who you are to look more impressive. Be honest; you'll be happier.

People want to be recognized. They love to hear their names. For some reason, hearing their names gives them certainty that you care about them and that you know them. People like to do business with people who know them. So start paying attention to people and recognizing everybody using their names. Pay attention to who they are. Recognition costs you nothing. And it can gain you everything.

Be respectful of everyone. Prove to each customer that he or she is the most important person in the world. Be present; pay attention to your customers exclusively; listen to them; help them solve their challenges; and do whatever it takes to serve them. Respecting others starts with respecting yourself. Get good at being who you are at your best, so that you can be respectful of everyone you connect with.

Be attractive in the marketplace. They want to see that you're put together, that you have a great image in the marketplace. You have to look and act like a professional—including your clothes, your hair, your hygiene, everything about you. When you can look in the mirror and see that you are attractive and have a positive self-image, your customers will see it, too.

Be knowledgeable. You should know what's so great about your products—the features, the benefits, and why your dealership is the best one in the world. But sometimes a question comes up and you're stumped. When you don't know the answer, it's perfectly okay to say, "I don't know. I'll find out." Customers don't judge you on what you know or don't know. They don't care what you know. They care how much you care about them. When it comes to knowledge, you can never have enough. But if there's something you don't know, just acknowledge that and find out the answer when the opportunity presents itself. You'll find people respect you when you admit this because you are being honest and vulnerable. Being vulnerable gives others a chance to be understanding, and that boosts their connection to you.

Customers want a clean, safe, and comfortable environment. Have you ever walked into an establishment and immediately decided to walk out because something wasn't right? This happens to your customers, too. They have a keen sense of intuition that tells them when an environment isn't safe or clean—or it's just not where they want to be. What is your environment telling people about you? Make sure your image is safe, clean, and comfortable—especially for children and families.

All these expectations should be very easy for you to deliver when you're aware of what your customers want. So start paying attention to your overall appearance and how you treat people. When you exceed these expectations, you better believe your paycheck will go up.

Lagniappe—Deliver more value than price

There's a Louisiana word called lagniappe (pronounced "lan-yap"). Lagniappe means "extra". You don't just give what you said you were going to—you deliver more. One of the keys to successful selling is to give a little bit more. Go the extra mile. Under promise, and over deliver. Your customers won't expect it, and they'll leave knowing they're going to tell others about you. I wasn't expecting that restaurant manager to pay my whole bill. I expected her to pay for my sour cream. I certainly didn't expect a $25 gift card so I could come back. That manager gave lagniappe. She went above and beyond.

You need to pay attention to people that much. Impress the heck out of them. Find ways to deliver more than you promised. Do that, and I guarantee your business will go through the roof!

What do customers demand?

You just read through a long list of customer expectations. Like your sales steps, most normal folks cannot remember all 11 expectations. So let's chunk down all the customer expectations into four customer demands. These are four demands that customers want from you—that you can easily deliver.

1. A perfect product. I wanted my taco salad to be perfect. Your customers want their new cars to be perfect. Now you might be thinking, "Boudreaux, what planet are you on? There's no such thing as a perfect product." I know that. But that doesn't mean they don't want it. That's why you have to do a great job of Getting The Picture, so you can offer the closest thing to a perfect product that you have.

2. They want it NOW. Right this minute. They don't want to wait another second. So deliver it! I know you have to wash the car, inspect the car, change the oil, and all those things. So find out what the delivery time is, and tell the customer. Keep them up-to-date, and deliver in a timely manner. If you're running behind, tell them right away. If you're running ahead of schedule, don't say anything. Deliver ahead of schedule. That's called lagniappe.

3. A delightful experience. Who's responsible for a delightful experience? You are. Not your manager, not your service people—you. Fortunately, it's easy. You deliver delightful by being kind and courteous and showing you care, and being present and respectful so they feel special. Again—wrong planet! You can't always guarantee a delightful experience. Ah, but that's good news for you. Because when things don't go right, then you get to prove how amazing you are. Because at that moment you get to build loyalty—the same way the manager at that restaurant did. What she did was amazing because she showed that she cared about my experience. She cared whether or not I came back, so she could prove I was wrong in judging them so harshly. Take advantage of the less-than-delightful times. That's your time to truly shine.

4. Show you care. That manager created *more* than a satisfied customer with me. She created a loyal customer—a loyal customer who raves about the food and the drinks and the service and brings people in the door whenever I can. You can do that, too. But if you don't show you care, and you do nothing to fix what's wrong, then you're the worst company in the world. And it's not worth walking in your door. That's how people will judge you. And you better believe they'll tell everyone on Facebook, Twitter, Yelp, Foursquare, and anywhere else they can think of.

How do you show you care? When there's a problem, here's what you do.

- Own the problem—Say "It's my fault" and don't pass the blame.
- No excuses—Don't give testimonials of failure; just apologize.
- Fix it now—Make it right.
- Whatever it takes.

Just like my sour cream. If you show you care by owning the problem and fixing it, you will earn a loyal customer. And the business of our business is people. Earning loyal customers is part of building and maintaining lifelong relationships—the key to massive success in this business.

It all gets back to the rules of engagement. Make it work for the customer. Make it work for you. And be 100 percent honest and in integrity with yourself, your customer, and your dealership. You are judged by your worst day. So, be who you are at your best every day, and you will be happy, profitable, and proud of what you do.

Own it!

Okay, it's time to implement what you've learned in this chapter. Fill in the blanks with words from your I AM list. Once you get used to creating statements like these, you'll be able to pull qualities from your list on the fly—whenever you need them.

What qualities, characteristics, and values must I have so that I can treat everyone like royalty? Write your list, and then narrow it down to what will drive you.

I am _____   I am _____

I am _____   I am _____

I am _____   I am _____

I am _____   I am _____

I am _____   I am _____

I am _____   I am _____

I am _____   I am _____

I am _____, _____, and _____ so that _____.

What qualities, characteristics, and values must I have so that I can solve my customers' transportation needs and challenges? Write your list, and then narrow it down to what will drive you.

I am _____   I am _____

I am _____   I am _____

I am _____   I am _____

I am _____   I am _____

I am _____   I am _____

I am _____   I am _____

I am _____   I am _____

I am _____, _____, and _____ so that
_____.

BREAK THE RULES...WRITE IN THE BOOK!

_____

_____

_____

_____

_____

_____

_____

_____

_____

_____

_____

_____

_____

_____

_____

_____

_____

_____

_____

_____

_____

_____

_____

_____

_____

_____

_____

Chapter Five

COMMUNICATION

"Are you even worth listening to?"

H ave you ever been driving down the road and a song came on the radio that you instantly knew you didn't like? Even if you had never heard it before, you immediately changed the channel. You just knew at a deep level you were not going to like that song, and it wasn't even worth listening to. Why did you feel that way? What made you change the channel? Maybe it was the melody. Maybe it was the volume or the tempo. Maybe you just couldn't relate to the genre of music, whether it was hip-hop or country or classical.

Are you that song?

Are you even worth listening to?

You want to be the opposite of that song. Not only do you not want people changing the channel, you want them hanging onto your every word. You want them so connected to what you're saying that they don't even want to go to the bathroom because they might miss something.

Communication is part of "getting good at being you." If you're in sales, you're probably already a pretty good communicator. I want you to become an *excellent* communicator. I want you to not only know how to communicate effectively with others, I also want you to be able to read what they're *really* saying—even when they're saying something else with their words.

When I got into this business, my dealership spent a lot of money for a man to come in and teach us how to use the telephone. Now, I'd been using a telephone my whole life, and I thought I was pretty good at it. But this man said we were using it wrong. He said we had to do certain things when we were on the phone trying to make appointments, get referrals, or following up with a customer. The first thing we had to do was memorize these long scripts he gave us. I was new, so I figured he must know best. I looked at the script, and my friend sitting next to me looked at the script, and we both looked at each other and said, "I don't talk like this!"

So I asked the man, "We can change the words, right?"

He said, "These words have been psychologically tested so the customer will do what you want them to."

I thought to myself, *They've been tested in Louisiana? Are you sure? Maybe up north where you're from they talk like this, but we don't talk like this.* I wanted to be successful. I wanted to sell cars, so I tried to memorize the script. Even after I moved to Texas, I tried to do what the trainer said—learn the words, learn the words, words are important. I really tried. It just never felt right. Something was missing.

When I went back home to Louisiana, I noticed something. I noticed the way that people back home talked. They talked with their whole bodies. When they told a story about catching a fish, you *saw* that fish on the line. I watched my dad talk to customers at the drug store. He was animated, kind, funny, helpful, and do you know he never had to memorize a script or word track? He spoke from his heart. He was caring, compassionate, and helpful—no scripts necessary.

Later on, I discovered that this is how successful car salespeople talk. For you to be comfortable and successful in this business, you have to communicate at a higher level. You have to talk like you mean it. Because our business, the business of people, is about mastering the art of listening and helping. It's about communicating at a level that guarantees the customer will not change the channel on you.

7 Percent of your communication skills are words

The other 93 percent of communication is how you bring those words to life. How does that word *feel?* Oh! That word smells good! Man, look at the color of that word. It's beautiful.

Words are powerful when delivered with all the things necessary to make them POP!

I remember talking to my sister when we were little, and she said to me, "Do you ever just listen to the letter P? It goes pa, pa, pa. I love the letter P. Pa Pa Pa."

And I said, "Yeah, I like Rrrrr. R is my letter. Rrrrr… RrrrrRRRRR. That's got a real power to it. That letter says, *I got this!*"

You can pronounce letters with great articulation, but you know, some letters just feel good in the back of your throat, right? Rrrrrr…

So you've got to know that 93 percent of your communication is bringing letters and words to life. They have power, but you've got to make them sound like you mean it.

The same sentence can mean two completely different things, and sometimes we say one thing and mean something else.

"REALLY?" Going up an octave at the end shows curiosity and intrigue.

"Really!" Dropping an octave with an eye roll means you're calling bullshit.

Ever ask your partner, "What's the matter, honey?"

She says, "Uh, NOTHING!" Does she really mean "nothing," or do you call *bull* on her? (Perhaps you keep your comments to yourself, 'cause it's safer for you.)

When you're using scripts and word tracks that you've memorized, they may not resonate with you. Or they might come across as insincere because you have to think about what you're saying. Talk from your heart. It builds trust. It builds rapport. And it's so much easier. Study the script, and then make changes to it so that it accomplishes the goal and comes across as real to you. What you want to say already lives inside you. You already have the right words. So take the words you're trying to learn and make them your own.

Maybe you make some mistakes when you talk from your heart. So what? You're human—congratulations! It's better to be genuine and come across as sincere, than to memorize a script in your head and "sound like a car salesman." Be yourself, speak from your heart, and sell more.

What are the other 93 percent of your communication tools?

You know the techs in your service department? They have a big heavy-duty toolbox that they've spent tens of thousands of dollars filling full of tools for one purpose—to solve a customer's transportation needs. Technicians are constantly investing in new tools so that they can have the best tool to fix the problem. They wouldn't use a monkey wrench or vice grips to take off a tire, unless that's all they had. They use the best tool for the job, so they pull out an impact wrench and *Brrrap!* That tire is off in no time. The technician can fix that car really fast because he has the right tools.

Most salespeople think their tools are things like word tracks, scripts, process, and product knowledge. But that's just the beginning...

Salespeople have tools, too. Most of them are taught that their tools are things like word tracks, process and product knowledge. But you have so many more tools you could invest in and use to be more effective.

I want to introduce you to the tools in your communication toolbox. Sure, you've got words in there. But if words are all you use, you're missing out on a whole lot of other tools that might do the job better and faster. The good news is, you don't need to buy these tools. In fact, you can't buy them. You only have to develop them. Nurture them inside you. You have to find the tools that work with *your* body, *your* style, and *your* personality. It has to be natural.

Who you are is perfect. I don't want you to change and start talking like me, or your manager, or your sales trainer. You are brilliant, and you deserve to have a natural process and style that honors who you are. And it's not difficult. I promise. When you take the time to develop your communication toolbox, you're going to succeed faster. Because when you communicate at a high level in a way that works for your customer and yourself—and is honest—then people will trust you and your sales will increase.

Okay, let's learn about the tools you'll want to develop.

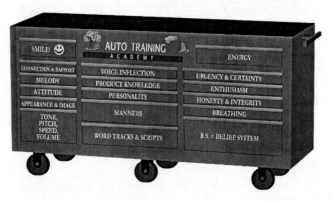

Use **all** *the tools in your communication toolbox to bring your selling skills to life so that you can solve your customer's transportation needs.*

1. Natural rapport

Have you ever been talking to someone you barely know and suddenly they get real quiet...and they say something like, "I don't even know why I'm about to tell you this, but..." and then they drop a deep, dark personal secret about their past on you?

Have you ever walked up to a customer on the lot who gave off a vibe or said to you, "Leave me alone. I'm not talking to any salesperson!"? They don't want to talk to you, trust you, or even be around you…and then two hours later, they're happily putting $2,000 down on a vehicle they didn't even plan on buying that day?

Have you ever noticed someone who just seems to have the magic touch with people? She can charm the socks off the grouchiest person and everyone she connects with loves her.

You want to know how they do it? It's just a strategy they're running. It's called rapport; and it's what makes people instantly like or dislike you, whether you know it or not. You get rapport by appealing to people's subconscious minds. And the way you connect to their unconscious minds is by acting, speaking, mimicking, mirroring, and matching everything about their communication skills. You can match how they're standing, how they're breathing, how they're talking, or their tonality. Everything you notice, make sure you're matching them. When the unconscious mind picks up on that, it sends a signal that says, "This person is a lot like me. I can trust them."

It's called Mirror Match, and it's taught all the time in the sales world. Mirror Match is a strategy for instantly connecting and creating rapport. It's used in psychology, neurolinguistic programming, sales, and politics. The challenge with this strategy for me is that it feels like I'm using it to manipulate people. I don't like to feel manipulative. I like to be myself.

How do you connect with people naturally, without focusing on Mirror Match or any other artificial tactic? Why is it that people connect with you so easily? How is it that you gain rapport instantly? Second graders do this naturally. They are the greatest connectors in the world.

Watch how they talk to each other. What do second graders do that makes you pay complete attention to them? *They're present.*

The way to be in rapport with someone instantly is to be 100 percent present with that person in the moment. It's like you put a cloak around the two of you and there's nothing else in the world that matters except that person. Be present. Don't look at your phone or check your messages while you're talking to someone. Don't look around at the other people near you. Be present. That person is the only and most important person in your universe at that time. When you're on the phone with someone, be present there, too. It should feel like the two of you are in the same room, even if you're half a world away.

The next piece to gaining rapport naturally is respect. Respect that person fully and listen. Respect them enough to ask questions so you can solve Problems or move toward new Possibilities. Presence + Respect = Instant Rapport. Without thinking, without matching their breathing or speech tonality, and without manipulation of any kind—they will naturally connect with you. They will trust you, and you already know how to do this naturally.

What makes you likable? That's more than rapport. That's kicking it up a notch. To be likable, you need presence, respect, and try adding in *happy.* Bring joy to your relationships. Once you become aware that the reason people like and trust you is because you are present, respectful, and happy—relationships and connection will flow effortlessly.

2. Voice inflection

I first became aware of voice inflection from Zig Ziglar, a master at teaching communication. He taught me that the way I deliver the words I speak is as important as the words themselves. The inflection of my voice is a major reason why people either understand what I'm saying or come away with the wrong idea. Here's how Zig taught voice inflection. Read the sentences below out loud. Any word that's italicized should be read louder and with more emphasis.

I didn't say he beat his wife.

I didn't say he beat his wife. (Someone else said it.)

I didn't *say* he beat his wife. (I implied it, but I didn't say it.)

I didn't say *he* beat his wife. (Someone else did it.)

I didn't say he *beat* his wife. (He gave her a spanking.)

I didn't say he beat *his* wife. (He beat someone else's wife.)

I didn't say he beat his *wife*. (He beat his dog.)

This is kind of a depressing example, but do you see how the same sentence read with different inflections can mean seven completely different things? If you read the sentence with no inflection at all, it's up to the listener to figure out what you're trying to say. There's no telling how many will get your meaning correctly. All you have to do is put the em-PHA-sis on a different syl-LA-ble and it sounds completely different. ☺

In addition to emphasis, you can also vary whether you end on an up octave or a down octave. That just means you end the sentence on a high or low inflection. Here's another example. Read the two words below as noted:

Up octave: "Really?" (Holy cow, I can't believe it! How awesome!)

Down octave: "Really?" (Wow. You really expect me to believe that? You must be out of your mind.)

So how can you use inflection to better communicate with your customers? Listen to yourself speak, record yourself on your cell phone, and then go back and listen. Are you emphasizing the right words? Are your customers getting the right picture from your words? If not, try adjusting your inflection and bring your sentences to life.

3. Melody, tone, pitch, speed, and volume

Have you ever listened to someone who speaks in a flat, monotone voice? Did you remember anything he said? Not likely. You probably fell asleep, or at least your brain did. Have you ever heard someone speaking very loudly using the same note? Did it appear that they might be yelling? Melody is the sing-songiness that comes across as pleasant or entertaining as opposed to yelling or anger. Melody helps you learn and remember. The best way to learn is to hear something and then repeat it with ridiculous melody. Let me prove it:

ABCD… You're singing it in your head, aren't you? That's okay, melody helps you learn and remember.

ABCDEFG… HIJKLMNOP…QRSTUV…WXY and Z… Now I've said my ABCs…

Did you sing it in your head? You probably learned the ABCs by using melody.

In addition to melody, you also have the tools tone, pitch, speed, and volume. Varying the way you say different sentences makes a big difference. For example, when you end a sentence or a thought, does your voice go up or down? Most likely, you finish a sentence ending with a period on a down beat. That's because it's how you were taught to talk. The down octave signals the end of a thought. But when you're communicating with customers, you don't want them to ever feel like it's over. You want them to hang on your every sentence—just waiting for your next brilliant idea. The way you do that is by finishing your sentences on an up beat instead of a down beat. When your words end on an up beat, the listener is hanging on, waiting for the rest of your thought. This is exactly what the media does. Listen to them. Before they go to a commercial, they'll use a cliffhanger in the form of a question (up note) or an incredibly interesting part of a story that you cannot miss so you feel like you have to hang on until after the break.

Breaking News—Special Alert—Do not miss this! They are selling you urgency, importance, and Oh My God, pay attention!

And you hook right in.

These are not questions, so they don't go up octave and they don't drop octave. Breaking News is done using the same note with a *commanding* tonality. You will do this!

It's your job to communicate so that your customers can experience an emotional attachment between what they want to buy and what you can do to help them. When you're leading a product presentation, for example, you want the customer to fully experience the vehicle—to feel, smell, notice, imagine, and picture themselves with an attachment to a better vehicle. Get all of their senses in the game.

For example:

See this (point to the amazing navigation system).

Touch this (go ahead and use the touchscreen to find your destination).

Feel this (feel how buttery soft the leather seat is on this vehicle?).

Notice this (notice how smooth your new vehicle rides on the highway).

Imagine that (imagine pulling up to your kids school and seeing how excited they're going to be).

Smell this (breathe in…there's nothing better than the smell of a new vehicle).

How can you use these tools to hold people's attention? How can you use melody to do your job better? You start just by being aware that melody is a wonderful tool to use whenever it feels appropriate. It helps to hear examples, too, so I've recorded several sales-based audio tracks for you. All you have to do is go to http://AutoTrainingAcademy.com/chapter-5-audio and have a listen. You want to communicate at a higher level with your customers, right? You want to easily and naturally sell more cars, don't you? Okay. Visit the website and watch and listen to what a huge difference melody, tone, pitch, speed, and volume will make for every prospect you talk to.

Breaking News!!! (same note with a commanding tone) This just in… The audio does not help people who don't go to the website and watch it. Do it now. ☺

4. Body language and posture

Have you ever walked up to a customer who really didn't want to talk to you, and in 10 seconds you've got a connection? How about the reverse? Have you ever had someone walk up to you, and you just *knew* you needed to get the heck away from them? Why does that happen? Is it something they said? Probably not. Most likely, it was their body language and their posture, or the way they held themselves. Body language can speak louder and faster than words. It can either connect you with someone instantly, or it can repel them equally as fast. What you do with your body is more important than what you say with your words.

You can learn to understand body language easier when you're aware of your own. The best way to learn body language is to pay close attention to other people's posture and body positions. Then put yourself in the same position, and ask yourself, *If I were sitting, breathing, looking, being like this, what would my body language be saying at that moment?*

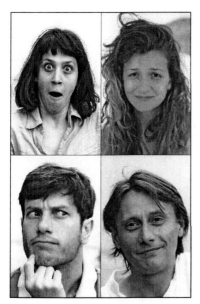

What thoughts and emotions are being communicated here?

Let's try it right now. Take a look at the following pictures. Stand up (really do it, now, no cheating) and mimic that position. How do you feel? What are your thoughts? Mimic the picture exactly, including the facial expression.

Now, go watch other people at the mall or some other large group. Put yourself into some of the different postures you witness, and see how you feel. Do the postures match what's coming out of their mouths? It's amazing how often people will say one thing with their mouths, while their bodies are saying something totally different. You might hear, *It's too expensive* or, *I can't afford it.* But the body is screaming, *I want to get it!!* Their words only represent 7 percent of what they're thinking and feeling. Their bodies tell the rest of the story. To read other people's body language, be aware of yours first. Put yourself in their shoes, and their heads. You'll be amazed.

5. Smile!

People's emotions are driven by their physiology. Want to be happy on the inside? Then be happy on the outside—SMILE. You can say almost *anything* with a smile on your face and get away with it. Go ahead and try it. Read these sentences out loud (and feel free to replace the word "jerk" with your favorite expletive).

Smile: Don't be a jerk with me, man.

No smile: Don't be a jerk with me, man.

It's the same sentence, but the energy of the experience changes when you lose the smile. Smile or no smile—it causes people to judge you and come up with their own ideas about who you are and whether they want to do business with you. With a smile, you can say amazing things to help people and influence the way they think, feel, and act. A smile, when properly administered, is one of the simplest and most appreciated gifts you can give.

6. Energy

Want to learn how to create high levels of vibrant and sustainable energy? In his brilliant book, *The Charge*, Brendon Burchard shares with his readers the formula for a charged life. I highly recommend it. Consider this analogy: a power plant doesn't *have* energy—it *creates* energy. Your body is the same. It doesn't have energy—it *generates* energy for you to use whenever you want it.

You can choose to be energized and alert whenever you want just by what you are thinking or doing. Even when you think you're worn out, you can summon energy (without the energy drink). I'll prove it to you. Have you ever been driving down the road minding your own business when all of a sudden you hear a siren? You look in the rear-view mirror and see the beautiful, shiny blue lights of your local police. Pulled over by the Po-Po. Has that ever happened to you? And did you have an instantaneous shift in energy? I'm going to guess you did. You changed in an instant because your body generated the energy it needed to deal with a potentially threatening situation.

You have the ability to summon energy like this all the time. You just have to be aware of how to do it. You have to put your body in a positive state, so you can generate energy on command. When you learn to control your energy, you can learn to influence the energy with customers, managers, and anyone you come in contact with. Do you think being more energetic will help you sell more cars? You better believe it will!

I have a couple of simple and amazing exercises I use to raise and maintain my energy levels. Would you like to learn them? (Say yes.) I have a demonstration video for you on the website. Just go to http://AutoTrainingAcademy.com/energy-levels/ and try them. You'll love how fast and easily you can boost your energy on the spot without depending on caffeine, sugar, and energy drinks.

7. Honesty and integrity

You've heard me talk about honesty over and over because it's one of the keys to Simple Selling. From a communication standpoint, anytime you tell a lie, you are fighting your body's unconscious natural behavior, which is to be truthful. When you tell the truth and you're not concerned about watching your words, you will communicate with more power and influence. You will be more inspiring to people around you. Don't think your customers won't notice dishonesty. At some point, they will. And as soon as you're caught in a lie you begin to lose your edge. Being authentic is critical to successful communication.

8. Knowledge

We talked about this in the last chapter about customer expectations. You don't know it all. And that's okay. Get the knowledge you need. Just realize it's perfectly okay to say, "I don't know. I'll find out." Be honest about what you know or don't know, and it will be appreciated. Want to know how you can easily remember all the product knowledge you'll ever need? Hang on til chapter 7, and I'll show you.

9. Manners

When I was young, every Sunday after church my six brothers and sisters would sit down to dinner with my parents. (Dinner is lunch in Louisiana. We eat supper at supper time.) Mama would make us eat like the bishop was coming to dinner. He never did, but we still had to learn how to use the right fork. We still had to cut our meat one piece at a time. We learned not to talk with our mouths full. I never thought it would serve me in life; but it turns out having good manners is incredibly valuable. Etiquette is incredibly fun to learn, too, even if you are just starting out learning it as an adult. Your manners communicate how you are and what you are and if you have class and if you're even worthy of being around. Whether you know it or not, people judge you (sometimes harshly) based on your manners.

10. Personality

Just be who you are. Be. Who. You. Are. Even if people laugh at you. Even if they make fun of you. When I was a kid, my classmates made fun of my dad because of his personality. Dad showed up passionately, playing full out with no regard for what anybody thought about him. He was noticeable. It wasn't until I was older that I realized how amazing he was, and how crazy I was for being concerned about what others said about this great guy. Accepting and embracing your personality is a powerful way to communicate more effectively. I challenge you to start being more personable. Your personality comes out in everything you do. My personality includes my Cajun culture, my accent, my quirky mannerisms, my passions, the way I dress, and the way I walk. All of those things add to my personality. My energy and frequency levels add to my personality. My presence adds to my personality. Your personality is about so much more than just the way you act or talk. Think about all the different aspects of your personality. Are you portraying the person you truly are at your best? Or do you need to shift and grow some behaviors or your appearance so that your personality matches who you are? Be proud of who you are. Accept, embrace, and grow your unique personality.

11. Attitude

Attitude is about your characteristics—who you are at your best. When you connect with the identity that you wrote on your list, it's highly unlikely you'll have a bad attitude. Because *that person* on the list is smart, kind, thoughtful, strong, productive, and happy. That person has a great attitude! And that person is you.

People with a great attitude aren't saying negative things about themselves. The goal is for you to be able to manage your own attitude. Your manager is not responsible for your state of mind. If he responds in a negative manner to something you did—that's on him. Just because he appears to be yelling by speaking loudly, using only one note, does not mean he's saying you're not doing your job right. (Sounds to me like he just might be melody challenged. ☺) Don't let it affect you. Take the raw data and figure out how to solve and serve. Use feedback to figure out how to make things work for your customer, yourself, and your dealership. Attitude is an inside job. You generate it just like energy. Keep your positive attitude throughout the day, no matter what happens on the outside.

110 | **KEEP IT SIMPLE SELLING**

12. Enthusiasm

Another characteristic of an unstoppable and bold second grade salesperson is enthusiasm. There is nothing more contagious than raw enthusiasm. Whether it's from a second grader trying to get the new video game or the mob trying to overthrow the government, *enthusiasm moves you*. Ever watch someone with incredible potential who stays below average or struggles? Potential without enthusiasm or desire is a recipe for average—because you can't teach passion, desire, or enthusiasm. You can teach tactics and strategies, but they'll only work if the student has the drive to get the result. I'm terrible at organization, but I'm *passionate* about helping people solve their Problems and get the cars they want. Guess what? I can sell a lot more cars with my enthusiasm than I could with my organization.

13. Urgency and certainty

Urgency and certainty coupled with enthusiasm and energy are the primary ingredients found in second graders, as well as brand new salespeople who sell to almost everyone they talk to at first. Add belief in the product, and you create a sales genius! Certainty definitely sells. The person who's the most certain always wins.

Sell or be sold. Someone is going to sell, and someone is going to be sold. Either you sell a car, or you're sold on the customer's story that they can't afford it. Either you sell a truck, or you're sold on the idea that they have to have the red one or it's no deal. Think about politics, for example. Have you ever listened to someone talking about politics, and they were absolutely *certain* about what was happening, no question about it. You watch that person and vehemently disagree. You know they are mistaken. But people are totally buying into what that person is saying. They are sold because of the passionate, unwavering belief of this individual.

Little children are *certain* if they don't have chicken nuggets *today* they're not going to enjoy life. You know it, too. So you go ahead and swing by the drive-thru. The next time your child asks to go to McDonald's, try giving a wishy-washy "no," and see what happens. Do they buy it? Or do they keep pushing because they know they've got a shot at changing your answer? *Whoever has the most certainty wins. Sell or be sold.*

14. Image and appearance

How you look is important. Make no mistake, you are judged by how you look. I used to have a nice black suit, and I wore white tube socks with it. Nobody ever told me you weren't supposed to wear white socks with a suit. I just thought they were socks. They protected my feet from my shoes. They kept my feet cozy. *They're socks. What's the big deal?* I thought. But people judged me on my appearance.

Jim Rohn said once, "To be attractive in the marketplace, first you must be attractive in the marketplace." You cannot look bad and have people be excited to work with you. Pay attention to your image, and the image of your facility. It goes back to the customer expectation of a clean, safe, and comfortable environment. Looks matter when it comes to communication. People will judge you on your looks before you even say a word.

15. Breathing

Most people breathe from their chests. But the correct way to breathe is called diaphragmatic breathing. That's just a long word that means breathe from your belly. Inhale and let the air go all the way down into your belly, let it expand, and then breathe all the way out. When you're communicating, take a breath in. Then as you're talking, your belly comes in slowly. You cannot breathe this way if you have bad posture. If you're slumped over or slouching, you won't be able to breathe correctly. So sit up tall, breathe properly. You will be rewarded with more energy, clarity, and better vocal quality. You'll be more powerful, you'll have more resonance. Breathing is also a powerful connector when it comes to rapport. It naturally connects you to other people.

16. The Perfect Voice—Roger Love

I've learned more about communication and its applications to selling from Roger Love and his program "The Perfect Voice" than anywhere else. Roger is recognized as one of the world's leading authorities on voice. His singing students range from The Beach Boys to John Mayer. His acting clients include celebrities like Reese Witherspoon and Joaquin Phoenix, as well as professional speakers like Anthony Robbins, John Gray, Suze Orman, and Dr. Laura Schlessinger. He also coaches many of the top Fortune 500 company executives. If you want to learn more from a master communication teacher, I strongly recommend you check out www.AutoTrainingAcademy.com/roger-love.

17. Proximity

This just means how close you are to someone else (or something else). Some salespeople like to get right up into the customer's personal space. What does the customer do? Usually, they are thinking, *Whoa! Back up buddy! You're in my space.* They don't feel comfortable, and it has nothing to do with what the salesperson said or how he looked or what he had for lunch. He was just standing too close.

How do you know when you're too close to others? Their bodies will talk to you, if you pay attention. One of the signals is that a person's foot will turn away from you. It's a subtle escape route they unconsciously developed to get away from you if necessary. When they are comfortably connecting to you, their feet may move up closer to you—saying *I'm in.*

If you're standing with a group of people, pay attention to the feet. You may notice that some of the feet are pointing in the direction of one particular person. In most cases, that's the influential, interesting, or attractive person that they want to connect with. (It's pretty freaky. Try it next time you're with a group of people you're getting to know.)

Another way to tell you're too close to people is to watch for a little gesture or a flinch. As you're walking toward them, they will have some small movement that gives it away. Maybe their eyes get bigger. Maybe they blink or look down. Maybe one of their fingers pops up. You'll see some movement that says *that's close enough.* They're not thinking about it; they just do it. If you're savvy enough to pick up on these clues, you'll know exactly when you've stepped "into their space." When that happens, be very present and respectful of where you are. All you have to do to set them at ease is take a step back.

On the other hand, if you want to totally shut others down, just step right up close to their face, on purpose. Their conscious minds will go into survival mode, and they won't be able to easily talk, think, or respond to your questions. Proximity is another important key to powerful communication and connecting.

18. B.S. = _____ _____

Not everyone appreciates the importance of B.S. when selling. I'll tell you, when I got really good at sales, it was because of B.S. No doubt. We all need a massive ration of B.S. in our lives every day. The right amount of B.S. will cause your paychecks to skyrocket. The right amount of B.S. will cause you to be so happy you're beaming. In case you're confused, B.S. stands for Belief Systems.

Let's talk about B.S. from a salesperson's perspective. When you first start a conversation with a potential customer, you should definitely believe you want to sell this person a car. Then you start asking questions to Get The Picture.

You: "What are you currently driving?"

Customer: "I'm driving a 2009 Chevy Aveo."

You: "Really? Did you buy it new or previously enjoyed?"

Customer: "Brand new."

You: "And when did you buy it?"

Customer: "I think it was around Christmas 2008."

You: "I see. And when is your next payment due on the car?"

Customer: "Uh…well, you see, I'm a little behind on my payments. Not too far behind, only 60 or 90 days. My bank is only calling me occasionally to track it down."

You: "No problem. And how much is your payment?"

Customer: "$712 a month."

You: "On an Aveo?! How did you get your payments so low?"

Customer: "I financed it for 72 months."

At this point, you're probably thinking, *Oh, no.* This guy has no money, no credit, he's not going to qualify for any type of loan. Do you still feel the same way you did 90 seconds ago? Do you still believe you're going to sell this person a car today? Of course not. You want to get away from that person as fast as you can.

In 90 seconds, you moved from a YES to a NO way!

Now let's look at it from a potential customer's point of view. The customer comes onto the lot thinking, *NO, I am NOT buying today. I'm just looking, came in to get a brochure and then leave.* Most customers come into your store with a great big NO in their heads.

But then you start asking questions to Get The Picture of what they are hoping for. You start to see what Problems they're moving away from, and what Possibilities they're moving towards. So you keep asking questions.

You: "So, what do you like most about your Aveo?"

Customer: "Oh, man, the gas mileage is off the charts!"

You: "I'm with you. It's like that little car just sips gas. I love that! What else do you like about it?"

Customer: "My wife loves it."

You: "That's so important! What is it she likes so much about it?"

Customer: "Well, my wife is one of those socially-conscious, vegetarian, hippie chicks, and she thinks we're protecting the environment together."

You: "That's wonderful. What else do you like about it?"

Customer: "Not a dang thing. I'm sick of that car!"

You: "You are? What don't you like about it?"

Customer: "Everything. I miss my truck! My whole life, I had a truck."

You: "Why in the world did you sell your truck?"

Customer: "Gas got to $4 a gallon. I couldn't keep both my wife and my truck. One of 'em had to go!"

You: "What else don't you like about the car?"

Customer: "There's no room in that thing. I used to have so much space to carry things in my truck. You can't fit hardly anything in the back of an Aveo."

You: "Anything else you don't like about your car?"

Customer: "You ever pull up to a fancy restaurant in a little car like this? It's embarrassing! I need a man's vehicle."

After you talk to the customer a little while, he starts to think more positively about a newer vehicle. He starts to move from *NO, I'm not buying* to believing *YES, I would consider something.*

IMPORTANT: What I'm about to share with you will make selling easier. You'll want to add it to every deal!

Sell or be sold.

With most salespeople, after about 90 seconds of asking the customer questions, this is what happens:

Salesperson is thinking: "OH NO. Go on, git, you can't buy your mama's love. This is a total waste of time. I need to get a real customer."

The customer is thinking: "YES! Please help me. I need my truck. I can't live with this little car another day. Please! I'll even pay for something I like."

At the beginning of a deal, the salesperson goes from YES to NO and the customer goes from NO to YES. That's lunacy.

Now here's the dirty little secret of great salespeople and managers in our industry: *They never leave YES. They believe in the deal.*

It doesn't matter what the customer said about his credit or his job. It doesn't matter if they want to buy the car or don't want to buy the car. Great salespeople believe in the deal. They believe in every deal, and then they kick it up a notch. They are creative, flexible, and resourceful. They do whatever it takes and then find the deal. They Get The Picture, discover the PP (Problems/Possibilities), and then they use that PP to help them close the deal. *They do not give up on a deal.*

It takes three people to believe in the deal. The customer has to believe, your manager has to believe, and somewhere in there we need a rock—someone who is never going to waver in their belief that a deal is going to happen. *That's where you come in.* Even if the manager doesn't believe, and the customer doesn't believe, you must believe. You must believe in every deal, be the rock—and when it's necessary, you have to be willing drag both your customer and your manager to a car deal.

You remember a time when you knew you had a deal. No doubt about it. There was no way this deal was not going to happen. The customer didn't believe, your manager didn't believe. But you believed, and you made the deal. How did that happen? *You had no doubt.*

How about the customer you believed couldn't or wouldn't buy? *No doubt about it. The customer goes to the next dealership and buys.*

What changed?

Your beliefs.

Both of those situations happen because of your BS—your Belief System.

So here's what I'm selling you. You've got to BELIEVE. Believe in the deal. Believe in yourself. Believe in your product. Believe in your customer. Believe in your company. Believe in your manufacturer. Believing in the deal will help you sell more vehicles and is one of your keys to success.

Need more proof?

Do you remember a time when you were in the zone? When everyone was saying YES!? I guarantee you believed you were going to sell EVERYONE. It didn't matter if they had bad credit, no credit, were upside down in their trade, or their spouse wasn't with them. You still believed.

How about the new salesperson? The first 90 days, they're selling EVERYONE. Why? Because they believe everyone is going to buy. Their belief system is off the chart!

Then after 90 days, they discover all the reasons people don't buy. Upside down. No credit. Bad credit. Newer vehicle. Spouse not present. They suddenly have all these reasons NOT to believe in the deal. And suddenly, they stop selling cars. It's not because they got their dealer's license; it's because they quit believing.

If we treat people like shoppers, they will shop. If we treat people like buyers, they will buy. It's all BS.

Own it!

Okay, it's time to implement what you've learned in this chapter. Be sure to visit http://AutoTrainingAcademy.com/chapter-5-video/ where you'll find bonus videos and examples for how to read body language, check your proximity, and practice your voice inflection, melody, and tone.

Next, fill in the blanks with words from your I AM list.

What qualities, characteristics, and values must I have so that I am a powerful, engaging, and influential communicator? Write your list, and then narrow it down to what will drive you.

I am _____   I am _____

I am _____   I am _____

I am _____   I am _____

I am _____   I am _____

I am _____   I am _____

I am _____   I am _____

I am _____   I am _____

I am _____, _____, and _____ so that

_____.

What qualities, characteristics, and values must I have so that I am definitely worth listening to? Write your list, and then narrow it down to what will drive you.

I am _____   I am _____

I am _____   I am _____

I am _____   I am _____

I am _____   I am _____

I am _____   I am _____

I am _____   I am _____

I am _____, _____, and _____ so that
_____.

What qualities, characteristics, and values must I have so that I have massive amounts of energy and enthusiasm? Write your list and then narrow it down to what will drive you.

I am _____   I am _____

I am _____   I am _____

I am _____   I am _____

I am _____   I am _____

I am _____   I am _____

I am _____   I am _____

I am _____, _____, and _____ so that
_____.

BREAK THE RULES...WRITE IN THE BOOK!

_____

_____

_____

_____

_____

_____

_____

_____

_____

_____

_____

_____

_____

_____

_____

_____

_____

_____

_____

_____

_____

_____

_____

_____

_____

_____

Chapter Six

LIFELONG RELATIONSHIPS

"No more one night stands."

Get good at being you—and loving, caring for, and helping people—a simple recipe for success. In chapters 3 through 5, we focused on you and your brilliance. Next, we move to the people part of your business. The business of your business is people, and the key to massive success is to master the art of building and maintaining lifelong relationships. That's what I did; I moved from the car business to the people business. It was simple, natural, profitable, and fun.

Your relationship tree is full of people. Building and maintaining relationships is about connecting with anyone, anywhere, anytime.

Imagine an apple tree

Picture a big, huge apple tree just full of apples. Some of them are green, some are just starting to ripen and turn red. Your dealer is going to throw hundreds of thousands of advertising dollars at that tree, hoping to shake it hard enough that some of the apples fall off and roll into the dealership. Your manufacturer is throwing hundreds of millions of dollars at the tree, praying that the apples fall off and stay loyal to their brand. Finally, the salesperson, waiting by the phone, the Internet, or the front door of the dealership, is hoping for the opportunity to have a shot at grabbing an apple—a customer. They hope maybe they'll sell a car. The majority of salespeople in our industry are filled with hopeium that the customer will buy today.

Here's what's really happening. Before you even get an opportunity to talk to the apple (the customer), gets bruised and abused from every direction. The customer goes to websites and blogs and eventually pulls into a dealership and talks to a salesperson. Now that salesperson asks a bunch of questions—you know, to Get The Picture of what the customer is trying to accomplish. The salesperson realizes the customer is not going to buy a car today. So he thinks, *Hmm, how can I make it tougher for the next salesperson? I know what I'll do, I'll low-ball the customer. I will tell the customer he can buy my vehicle for $1,000 back of invoice. And I'll kick it up a notch, and tell them about a great incentive program that doesn't even exist.*

The customer leaves that dealership a little bruised up. He goes to the next dealership, and the next salesperson picks up the apple and starts asking a bunch of questions—you know, to Get The Picture and discover the PP (Problems and Possibilities). This salesperson realizes that the customer is not going to buy a car today, and even if he did, he couldn't make any money on it. So, the salesperson thinks, *What can I do to mess the customer up even more?* And this salesperson decides he'll tell the customer his trade-in is worth several thousand dollars more than the Blue Book value on it. That customer leaves the dealership all messed up, more bruised. Ever had a customer like this? Then the customer goes to another store where nobody waits on him. He's totally ignored. So he leaves frustrated and goes to the next store—yours. You're the next salesperson.

I don't know if you've had this customer before or not. Chances are you've had someone come into the dealership who has been misled and lied to. The result is you make no money, or you get mini-deals. You lose credibility with the customer. It's like there's a disconnect. It may even seem confrontational—not just with the customer, but also with your manager. You feel like everybody is beating you up—the customer, your manager, and your competition. You end up struggling and have a bad month. You're obviously in the wrong business; this just doesn't fit.

Here's the lunacy: the dealer gives you inventory, training, technology, management support, clerical support, tons of resources—and for some reason as salespeople, we have decided that the best way for us to do our jobs is to wait for the next apple to come into our store in the form of a floor Up, a phone Up, or an Internet lead. That's crazy!

There are salespeople in our industry who have had neighbors buy from other salespeople at the same dealership. They've had friends buy the same type of car from somebody else they don't even know at another dealership. They've had relatives buy from someone else. All because we have decided that the best way to do this business is to wait for the apple to fall off the tree and roll into the store.

Successful salespeople don't do business that way. Successful salespeople climb up the tree, and get in amongst the apples. They talk to everybody they know. They touch every apple. Their focus is on *their* tree, not whatever tree the dealer is throwing money at this week. Successful salespeople are connected to all the apples in their trees. When an apple gets ripe, it falls right into the salesperson's hand, and they gently place it in their monthly basket.

Those apples are *people,* and they never get ignored, mistreated, or talked down to in any way. They go straight from the tree to the hand to the paycheck. Profitable salespeople know that the business of this business is *people*. And the key to massive success is not just building relationships (anybody can do that), but it's *maintaining* those relationships for life. It's staying connected, and staying in the service mode.

So how do they do it?

It all starts with your relationship tree. You have to learn to recognize and connect with your current relationships. Where can you bring value to these people? This is not about selling. It's about connecting. It's about likeability. It's about helping whoever's in your tree with whatever they need.

Whether you know it or not, you have a massive relationship tree. In your tree, you have childhood friends who you've known forever. You have new friends—some you've known just a few years. You've got previous co-workers, your family, and your partner's or spouse's family. You might have participated in sports or another hobby; there are relationships there. You have relationships through school—your school and your children's schools. Your children's activities like cheerleading, football, soccer, math club, speech club—there are relationships there. Get to know the parents of the other children. Get to know the teachers who run the activities. Gas stations and grocery stores—there are people there; build a relationship with them. Restaurants—got a favorite one? Start building relationships there. These are all people you're connected with in your tree. Social groups—are you active in politics? Do you go hunting or fishing with other people? Are you a member of a civic group like the Rotary Club, Kiwanis, or Lions? Do you play cards with people once a week? Maybe you go to casinos, or you like to go dancing. At your own dealership, you have co-workers and vendors who come and go. You have Facebook and other social media. The list of possibilities goes on and on.

1) Give Referrals - Be a Connector
2) Business to Business - Promoter
3) Service and Body Shop
4) Back of the House Mouse
5) Friends and Family
6) Church/Charities
7) Social Groups and Events
8) Children's Activities
9) School
10) Personal Marketing
11) Grocery Store
12) Internet Communities
13) Floor Ups/Phone Ups
14) Vendors

Think of all the places you can build relationships and treat people like royalty. The possibilities are endless!

All these places are where you can find your relationships. The people in these places are the apples in your tree. Remember, *the business of your business is people. And the key to massive success is to build and maintain lifelong relationships.*

Circle…Highlight… Pay Attention to this:
QUIT SELLING CARS!
There is no money in cars!

We can walk your lot and look at every car—pull the carpets out, check out the glove box, look in the storage pockets behind the seats—there's no money there. Money doesn't live in cars. *Money lives with people.* People give you money to get the car. Quit thinking you're in the car business. You are in the people business. That's where you want to be.

To be successful, you must figure out how not only to connect with your tree, but also how to *grow* your tree. You have to possess strategies to connect with people anywhere, any time. You have to know what makes great conversation when you're waiting in line at the post office or Starbucks. There are so many places to meet people. But you need words and strategies.

What to talk about

People love to talk about themselves. It's their favorite subject. So, your best strategy is to get them talking about themselves in some way. You can ask what kind of music they like, or their favorite food. Or do they enjoy sports? Do they like to play the game or watch? What's their favorite team?

What do they do for a living? There's a powerful thing to talk about. Find out what their occupation or their business is. Then learn more about it by asking questions—you know, to Get The Picture. How's their business going so far this year? How did they get into that business? What demographic makes up their best customers or clients?

Why would you ask questions about *their* businesses? Here's why. One of the ways we've been taught to connect with people in this business is to *ask for referrals*. Dealers have spent hundreds of thousands of dollars over the years on trainings to teach salespeople how to ask for referrals using word tracks and scripts—knowing that *when we ask, we get*. But we don't ask. Here's why: it's not part of our natural behavior. Most salespeople will do more for somebody else than they will ever do for themselves. We don't feel like we've made enough emotional deposits to beg from a total stranger. So, we just don't ask. It's not part of our nature to beg, so we don't do it. We don't ask for referrals unless it's easy and fits who we are.

How do you get referrals without asking for them?

Since you have a relationship tree, then it makes sense that everyone in that tree has their own relationship trees. They have people in their trees who will have a transportation need at some point, whether it's sales or service or just getting expert advice. They could refer those people to you, if they choose to. But before they do that, they need to know they can trust you and that they will have no regrets for sharing that relationship. So do something good for those people. Show them with your actions that they can trust you and that you won't let them down or embarrass them if they refer people to you. The way you get referrals naturally is to *serve* each relationship. *Give* referrals first by becoming a connector of relationships, and you will naturally get referrals in return. There are two ways to get referrals: by asking and by giving.

Here's an example. Let's assume you have 800 relationships in your CRM (Customer Relationship Management database), and one of those people owns a pizza parlor—Antonio's Pizza. You've maintained the relationship with that person; you've been to his restaurant and like eating there. What if you went to the owner and said, "Antonio, would you mind if I told 800 of my closest friends how great your restaurant is?" Of course he's going to say that would be wonderful. Can you imagine sending an email out to your entire relationship tree and telling everyone how great Antonio's pizza is? You might also tell them your favorite dishes and how well Antonio treats people. What you're doing is bringing value to Antonio. Why? Because Antonio also has a relationship tree. If you serve him first by sending your relationships to his restaurant, then he will see that he can trust you may be able to reciprocate. The next time someone in his tree needs a car, who do you think he'll refer them to? You!

It works the same way with anyone in your tree. Someone in your tree might build gorgeous custom cabinets, and you find out someone else in your tree needs new cabinets. Hook them up! Connect them! You're bringing value to two people at once. This is what relationships are all about. Giving and supporting and connecting people who have needs. That's all great salespeople do. They solve people's transportation needs. Giving referrals is about giving value. It's about promoting other people's businesses.

Other ways to grow your tree

Some experts say salespeople should work the service lane. That's not easy, because the service lane can be a war zone at times. Instead, work the service lounge. Go meet people who are waiting for their cars to be serviced. Again, this is not about selling. This is about connecting. It's about discovering whether this person has a need you or someone in your tree can help fill. When you work the service lounge, just get to know people. Offer them coffee or refreshments. Visit with them about their favorite subjects—themselves. Ask questions—you know, to Get The Picture. What type of work do they do? What are they currently driving? How long have they had it? Questions help you discover the PP (Problems and Possibilities) and let you know whether you can help them out. Build and maintain a relationship with everyone you meet. You never know how you might be able to help them.

Another place to grow your tree is in your own dealership. Get to know the people you work with. Salespeople sometimes have an aversion to getting to know people in the service department. For example, they would rather be the House Mouse and beg for scraps from the manager than get to know everyone else around them. It's more valuable to be the Back-of-the-House Mouse.

Don't just look to your manager for deals; look to the people in the business office, or the HR department, or the service department. You have a guy in service who spends $40,000 for a blue box with tools in it. He loves cars. On the weekends, he builds cars with his friends. And last week, you took in a trade that would be perfect for him and his friends to fix up to race. But you don't know that because you don't know him. You may think the techs don't like you, but they don't know you.

Everyone who gets to know you ends up liking you. So get to know the people in your store. How can you build relationships with everyone in your store? Zeigler Auto Group employees get to know their fellow co-workers by giving them notes of recognition known as Diamond Drops for doing a great job. I remember one time I stopped by the store to visit with a group of newly hired employees and share with them the exciting opportunities that existed as a result of doing a great job in this business. I was pleasantly surprised to get a couple of these Diamond Drops myself. Talk about a great way to get to know people! Tell your coworkers how impressed you were with something specific they did. Let your fellow coworkers know about the "friends and family" sales program just for the people who are employed at the dealership. Be the person in your dealership who people come to for help simply because you're charming and thoughtful and caring. Understand that the value of those relationships is greater than any car deal. Put people in a position where they have no regrets for introducing you to the folks in their trees. And when they do, you have to be grateful—not because you sold a vehicle to someone in their tree, but because they trusted you enough to connect you.

You can connect with people and build your tree in some other surprising ways. For example, if you have a wife or significant other who works outside the home, bring her flowers at her office once a month.

It's a good thing to do, but it's also a great way to connect. Everyone in that office is going to be curious about you, and talk about you, and talk to you once a month. That's pretty valuable. Think about how else you can use this idea. Maybe bring some chocolates to your aunt who works at the credit union. If you have an uncle or father who works at a big company, go visit them. They're going to brag about you. Connect with them. Bring a six-foot sub into your own service department, and show your appreciation.

Want some more ways to grow your tree? Here you go:

Church or charities. If you go to church, don't just show up for the services. Take some time before or after to fellowship with other members of the congregation. Get to know them. Help them out, if they need it. The most powerful thing you can do is *give* to those people in your church and in the community. Help the sick or the elderly, or be a part of the mission to feed the hungry. Being involved in your community is a good thing all on its own, but it also allows you to be seen by more people. It allows you to connect with more people. What could you be doing to connect with more people at your church or charity?

Cultural connections. It doesn't matter where I go, I am connected to anybody wearing a purple and gold shirt that says LSU Tigers. We have something in common. I am from south Louisiana. If you're of Cajun descent or have a name ending in -eaux, we're probably related. I have a natural connection to this cultural group everywhere I go. Where do you connect?

Events. When you go to events like a football game or the ballet or community festivals, do you attend, or do you participate? Events are a great way to connect with others. You can volunteer to sell concessions at your daughter's soccer game, or you could be an usher at your local theater company. The events in your life allow you to build your tree. People see you helping out and appreciate you. It's a good thing. What are some other events you attend where you meet other people?

Children's activities. Do you get to attend events because of your children? I'm talking about sports, dance, karate class, swimming, band concerts, or chess matches—all sorts of things. Children's activities are powerful—not just because you get to see your kid being awesome, but also because you have the opportunity to help other people and grow your tree. All those other parents and grandparents and neighbors are sitting right there. They all drive cars. Talk to them. Put them in your tree. When it's time for them to look for a new car, they're going to fall out of the tree and into your hand. Then all you have to do is put them into your monthly basket. What activities do the children in your life attend? How can you be more supportive of their efforts, and connect with more people at the same time?

Personal marketing. Great salespeople are always trying to find ways to personally market themselves. But let me tell you something—Facebook is not a marketing tool. It is a connecting tool. Social media is a great way to connect with others and talk about *your friends'* favorite subjects. Post pictures like *theirs.* Do not be the person in my feed who is always promoting himself. Be diverse on social media. Don't limit yourself to one topic like religion or pets or politics. Be somebody who talks about great things happening in lots of different areas. Have fun! And be social.

If you want to do business on Facebook, try taking a picture of a person with her new car and post it for them on *her* wall (not yours). Then just comment underneath saying, *"I hope you love your new car."* Everyone who sees that picture will see the new car and your comment.

Then just click the like button of all the good comments that follow. How can you be more engaged with other people on social media?

The grocery store. I am fond of grocery stores because I love to cook and I was once in the business. I was the assistant produce manager at George Theriot's Grocery. I made sure everyone I used to work with there knew where I worked after I left. I stayed connected. You never know when you can help out a former co-worker.

You need to create relationships with the people at your grocery store. Get to know everybody there—not to sell a car, but to connect with them. Talk about their families. Talk about their favorite subjects. Pay attention to the guy stocking cans in the soup aisle. Nobody talks to that guy unless they need to find the pasta.

When I moved to Houston, I shopped at the same Kroger's every week. I knew everybody there, and they knew me. Out of the blue one day, the meat manager runs up to me and says, "Oh my God, Boudreaux! You're in the car business, right? Can you help me? My ex-wife is about to let our Suburban be repossessed. She's two months behind, and it's going to hurt my credit. I'm not paying for her mistakes! Please, could you call her and see if you can get her out of that car? If it gets repossessed, they're going to come after me."

I said, "I would be happy to." Then he gave me a heartfelt warning about how bad she was to work with.

I called her up and said, "Hi. My name is Boudreaux, and I'm with the local Chevy store. I've been told you have a Suburban, and I wanted to know if you'd be interested in selling it. I think I may have a buyer for it."

She said, "Where did you get my name?"

"Well, your ex-husband used to have that vehicle, and I was talking to him about it."

She got all excited to talk to me then. "Well, I hate this Suburban. This was *his,* and I never really liked it. I would love to get rid of this Suburban, but I don't want to spend a lot of money."

I said, "I understand that. What would you be looking for to replace it?" We talked a little more, and it turns out she was looking for a little two-door sports car. Oooh, she knew exactly what she wanted—a fully-loaded little red car with a sunroof, leather seats, and a five-speed transmission. She was going to feel so good driving that. As she was talking to me, I got a picture of what Problem she wanted to get away from and what Possibilities she was hoping for. Then I said, "Well, I'm not sure if we have something exactly like that, but we do have a lot of sporty cars for you to look at. You don't have to buy anything anytime soon do you?"

"No. I don't have to get one at all," she said.

"When would be a good time to come down, this afternoon or tomorrow?"

She said, "This afternoon."

That afternoon, she came by the dealership and took a stroll around the lot, looking at all the cars that fit her picture. And sure enough, she saw a bright blue metallic car, almost exactly like the one she wanted. The only trouble was it didn't come with a standard transmission; it was automatic. So, I said, "Let's just take this one for a ride, and you can see how it drives."

Oh, she drove and fell in love with that car. And when I told her how much it cost, she had to be thinking, *Oh, this is so much better than that big old Suburban from the guy that I hate.* We made the deal, and she got the little sports car. Cha-ching!

Next, I filled out the bird dog referral slip for my friend the butcher. I went back to the grocery store all proud and handed him his check.

And he said, "You're paying *me?* I'm going to take care of you." He saw two rib eye steaks in my cart and he said, "Those look a little...old. I need to mark these down a bit." I rarely paid full price for meat at that store ever again, and it was all because I valued the relationships with everybody there.

Vendors. You have people being paid by your dealership to work there. Maybe they cut the grass or wash the windows. Get to know these people. Get them a cup of coffee. At some point, they may need service, or they may need to get a new vehicle. You're the connection at that store. Get to know *everybody* who comes to your dealership.

Whatever you do—whether you're into politics or the arts, whether you like indoor activities or outdoor activities, whether you're a poker player or involved in social groups, or you go to the gym—whatever you do and wherever you go, you can talk to people about what they're currently driving. Whatever you do and wherever you go, you can talk to people about what they do for a living. Whatever you do and wherever you go, you can talk to people about food, music, and life. *You want to be present and respectful. And you want to have joy and happiness.* That's what makes you likable. This is the key to success in the people business: building and maintaining lifelong relationships.

The Three Little Pigs

Once upon a time, there were three little pigs. The first pig built his business with straw, the second with wood, and the third built his business with bricks.

The first business was built with straw—it was based on talking to Ups. This business matched industry statistics and closed 20 percent of the customers who chose to do business with him. Here was his business plan: 3 Ups a day. He worked 5 days a week and spoke to 15

Ups per week. In 4 weeks, he spoke to 60 new people. That meant his business would sell 20 percent of 60 people or about 12 vehicles. Great plan, right?

The second business was built with wood—it was based on talking to confirmed appointments. This business also matched industry statistics for appointments and closed 40 percent of the customers who chose to do business with him. Here was his business plan: 3 appointments a day. He worked 5 days a week and spoke to 15 appointments per week. In 4 weeks, he spoke with 60 new people. That meant his business would sell 40 percent of 60 people or about 24 vehicles. Better plan, right?

Now, you get appointments from all sorts of places, so the second little pig didn't just limit himself to setting appointments from phone Ups or Internet leads. As you know, there are other places to get appointments. You get them from people you know, from people you just met, from your service department or service lounge, and from referrals. All of these are ways to get appointments. So, it doesn't matter if you don't get phone Ups at your dealership. You still have to be successful in spite of that.

The third business was built with brick. It was based on the little pig's relationship tree. This business also followed industry statistics for relationship-based sales and closed 70 percent of the relationships choosing to do business with him. Here was his business plan: 3 relationships a day. He worked 5 days and spoke to 15 friends per week. In 4 weeks, he spoke to 60 people who knew him. That meant his business sold 70 percent of 60 people or about 40 vehicles. Wow!

It's your choice. You can build your business with straw, sticks, or bricks. You can sell 20 percent, 40 percent, or 70 percent of the people you visit with on a daily basis. That's how it works. Every opportunity earns you money; every appointment earns you money; every relationship earns you money. It's all about relationships and talking to people. The more people you talk to, and the more often you talk to them, the more cars you sell. People, people, people.

Build your business with relationships, and you'll have a brick-solid strategy for living the good life.

Follow up—with everyone and for all the right reasons

There are all sorts of fears wrapped around follow-up. Follow-up might not happen if you're worried about the price, what you're offering for the trade, or if you think you already know why they're not going to like what you have to offer. It might not happen if you didn't have the right vehicle on the lot, or you couldn't get their credit to the right level, or you were on the wrong vehicle entirely. Whatever the reason, consider this: the person you hope to talk to today is not as valuable as the person you spoke with and started a relationship with yesterday. Follow up!

Three questions that eliminate follow-up reluctance

Before your next call, ask yourself these three questions. Find a way to get a yes on all three, and watch your fears turn to opportunity.

1. If the follow-up call helped the customer, would you make the call?
2. If the follow-up call worked for you, would you make the call?
3. If the call were 100 percent honest, would you make the call?

I'm sure you answered *yes* to all three. These are the Rules of Engagement. Remember? It works for your customer, works for you, and is 100 percent honest. You will make more calls if you frame your follow-up based on the Rules of Engagement. Everybody should be followed up with because that is the foundation for the relationship—communication, solving, and serving. Follow-up is nothing more than making sure you ask, "What can I do for you?"

It's about connecting. It's about talking to people. How do you earn money? *You talk to people.* Recurring conversations build recurring revenue.

Not everybody can buy (the most powerful part of this book)

As you know, not everybody can buy a car. Some people are a total waste of time. You want to get rid of them quickly. They could be upside down, or have bad credit. You know the person—you run a credit application on him and he has a 400 credit score with a 52 percent income-to-debt ratio. He can't put any money down. He's upside down in his trade, and it's got a transmission problem. He has a short term on his residence, and only 11 months on his job. You've had this customer. We call a customer like this a roach, a jerk, or a jack. I know you've heard these names before—a flake, a snake, a credit criminal, a mutt, a waste of time, a tater bug, a cash buyer, next!

One of my little girls was born premature at 2.9 ounces. She was tiny and not well. Her first 30 days of life were spent in pediatric ICU. After hundreds of visits to the hospital, we were on a first name basis with folks in the emergency room, intensive care units, and doctors' offices. Everybody knew us. Andrea was blind, could barely hear anything, and couldn't speak. When the crisis would begin and she started to get sick, her lungs would fill with fluid. Her skin would swell up and turn blue even with extra oxygen, and her whole little body would balloon up from fluids. Imagine hitting your hand with a hammer really hard, and it turns blue and starts to throb. Her whole body was like that. She was in extreme pain, which caused her heartbeat to increase dangerously for extended periods of time. She was basically drowning inside her own lungs. The doctors and nurses would poke and prod at her, twisting her little body, and that sent her heart beating even faster. Fight, desire, passion, love, will—whatever you want to call it—by some miracle, she would manage to come home once again.

The medical bills were insurmountable. The collection people sent me letters every day. I would get five or ten letters every day from people I could not pay. They would call me on the telephone, telling me they were going to file a judgment against me and ruin my credit. You think I cared about my credit? You think I'm a roach? A credit criminal?

At some point, my refrigerator broke and couldn't be repaired. I had $150 and an advertisement from a local appliance store saying if you had no credit, bad credit, no money down, but you had a job, that you would be approved. I went down to the store and picked out a modest refrigerator. I filled out the credit application. The salesperson saw how much money I made and how long I'd been in the car business. He figured it was a done deal, and he asked me if I wanted it delivered. I said yes. He sat me down in a cubicle, said he was going to take care of everything and to just wait a little bit and he'd be back. Then the salesperson didn't come back for a long time. I thought he was just getting the paperwork ready. People would walk by the cubicle where I was sitting, and I smiled and waved to them.

Finally, I wondered what was taking so long. I asked someone where my salesperson was, and they pointed to an office. I saw the people in the office with my big long credit report full of judgments and charge offs.

And they were laughing at me.

They were calling people over to look at my credit report.

People were leaving the office and walking by the cubicle I was in—curious to see what "somebody with credit that bad" looked like.

I was never so humiliated in all my life.

I felt worthless.

I wanted to crawl under the linoleum and sneak out of there.

I felt demoralized and I left swearing to never let that ever happen to me again.

That's how we treat people in this business.

We treat people horribly.

Am I a roach? A jerk? A jack? A flake? A credit criminal?

Or am I just a loving, caring dad on the magical misery tour of life?

Do I deserve these labels? To be treated like less than a human being?

Nobody told me how to manage this deal.

Nobody told me what it was going to take.

We treat people like shit in this business. Is somebody with an 800 credit score really a better person than someone with a 400? Are they a better mom or dad? Are they more caring or loving? Do they deserve more respect than others?

The manufacturers got involved in the 1980s because we didn't care enough about the customers. They started sending out letters to the customers asking them to grade us on how they were treated. Some dealers stuffed the mailbox so they got good CSIs and the manufacturers didn't have to talk to the customers. Because we didn't care; it was all about that deal that day. There was no consideration for the long term. After all, *it's the end of the month that counts—not people.*

Enough!

No More!

This must stop!

Do you think my dad or my Uncle Jerry in the drug store would ever treat you badly? No! They would never laugh at you or make fun of you because of your condition or because of something going on in your life. It's not part of their nature. It's not part of who they are.

It's not part of who you are either.

I'll prove it to you. Think back to a time when you first started in this business, and you were shocked, repulsed, or baffled by how we spoke about employees and customers. That's you. That's who you really are—the person who was appalled by how we treat people. That's the person who needs to be in this business.

Go back to your I AM list. Look at those words. Words like—

I am caring.

I am thoughtful.

I am considerate.

I am compassionate.

That's you. That's the person who will be successful. That's the person who can be proud of what he or she does...every day.

No more. No more negative labels. No more treating people horribly. It's time to treat *everyone* like royalty. Become an advocate. That's what great salespeople are—advocates for the customer. That's what relationships are built upon. Respect. You cannot respect somebody else, until you respect yourself. And once you respect yourself, you can't help but treat everybody better.

This industry is a gold mine. We deserve to have an industry that treats people like royalty—an industry that cares about everyone regardless of their ability to buy today. It's about relationships that last forever. In this lifetime, you or somebody you know will experience the magical misery tour that I was on. Don't you want somebody to be there? Somebody like you? Somebody who can proudly help them?

My challenge is for you to say, "Enough! Everybody deserves a delightful experience. I am going to fight for the customer, my industry, my brand, and my family—one relationship at a time."

That's what I'm selling you. The business of this business is *people*. The key to massive success is mastering the art of building and maintaining *lifelong* relationships. If you do that, you'll be profitable. And if you treat them with respect, like royalty, you'll be proud of what you do. You'll be happy with the day you just had. And you won't be able to wait for the next morning when you can do it again. When you can solve and serve and take care of people passionately in an industry, your business becomes about respect and trust.

It starts with you. It starts now. Congratulations!

Own it!

Okay, time to implement what you've learned in this chapter.

Any good salesperson can build relationships. The gold is in maintaining them over a lifetime. They require attention. Fortunately, most of the time you can maintain them while you're shopping, or going to the gym, or visiting your favorite restaurant, or hanging out at your kid's school. And it's pleasurable to maintain relationships.

Write down at least 50 places you can go to meet new people and build relationships. (It's okay to look back at the examples I gave you.)

_____	_____
_____	_____
_____	_____
_____	_____
_____	_____
_____	_____
_____	_____
_____	_____
_____	_____
_____	_____
_____	_____
_____	_____
_____	_____
_____	_____
_____	_____
_____	_____
_____	_____
_____	_____
_____	_____
_____	_____
_____	_____
_____	_____
_____	_____
_____	_____
_____	_____

Write down at least 25 businesses or organizations you can promote to build goodwill and foster relationships.

_____   _____

_____   _____

_____   _____

_____   _____

_____   _____

_____   _____

_____   _____

_____   _____

_____   _____

_____   _____

_____   _____

_____   _____

_____   _____

Write down at least 10 ways you can stand out just for being an awesome human being.

_____   _____

_____   _____

_____   _____

_____   _____

_____   _____

Fill in the blanks below with words from your I AM list.

What qualities, characteristics, and values must I have so that I can build and maintain lifelong relationships? Write your list, and then narrow it down to what will drive you.

I am _____   I am _____

I am _____   I am _____

I am _____   I am _____

I am _____   I am _____

I am _____   I am _____

I am _____   I am _____

I am _____   I am _____

I am _____, _____, and _____ so that
_____.

What qualities, characteristics, and values must I have so that I can be proud of what I do every day? Write your list, and then narrow it down to what will drive you.

I am _____   I am _____

I am _____   I am _____

I am _____   I am _____

I am _____   I am _____

I am _____   I am _____

I am _____   I am _____

I am _____, _____, and _____ so that
_____.

BREAK THE RULES...WRITE IN THE BOOK!

_____
_____
_____
_____
_____
_____
_____
_____
_____
_____
_____
_____
_____
_____
_____
_____
_____
_____
_____
_____
_____
_____
_____
_____
_____

Chapter Seven

KEEP IT SIMPLE SELLING

"Do whatever it takes to find the deal."

S elling, solving, and serving should come as easily as breathing. It should be part of your natural behavior. When it is, then our industry serves more people and creates more success stories. I'm about to reveal the heart of KEEP IT SIMPLE SELLING (KISS). Yes, it's a process. It works with any sales process you are currently using, and the best part is, you already know how to do it. It's natural. It's easy. You use it when you talk to your children. You use it when you go to the grocery store. You use it when you visit with a stranger at Starbucks. You've been doing it your whole life. KEEP IT SIMPLE

SELLING is going to help you sell more cars and take care of people throughout the dealership.

First, I want you to get a pen and do this quick exercise. Write the steps of your sales process in the spaces provided below. Write down all 10 or 12 or 18 steps you were taught; however many there are, just write them down. Do it as quickly as you can. When you have to stop and think for a second, you're done. Stop at that point. Write in the book!

Ready? Go!

1. _____
2. _____
3. _____
4. _____
5. _____
6. _____
7. _____
8. _____
9. _____
10. _____
11. _____
12. _____
13. _____
14. _____
15. _____
16. _____
17. _____
18. _____

Did you get them all right?

Was it easy?

Did you use something similar to this process in grade school?

Was your road to the sale easy to learn and remember?

Did you answer *No*?

Why can't you easily remember that 10-step process?

Selling processes can range from five steps up to 23 or so steps. Managers, dealers, general managers, and trainers who create these selling processes are passionate. They protect these commandments, and for good reason. A great sales process really does work. But when I ask a room full of salespeople and managers to list the steps of the sale in my seminars, fewer than five percent can remember them all. They go blank after the third or fourth step. Salespeople unconsciously see the steps every day in the conference room and still don't remember them. Is it because they are unprofessional? Apathetic? Ignorant? None of the above!

7 (+ or -) 2

In 1956, the cognitive psychologist, George Miller, from Princeton University, published a paper stating that the conscious mind can only keep track of seven, plus or minus two, of anything before it has to consciously think about it. (That "plus or minus two" means there's a range between five and nine.) When asked to list items of any kind, you'll get to seven, plus or minus two, and you'll notice that your eyes shift and you'll think, "Uhhh…. What else?" This has come to be known as Miller's Law.

You've been watching cereal commercials since you were a child. You and your kids may have some favorites. Right now, list off as many breakfast cereals as you can, and say them in your head. You'll notice that you'll get to seven, plus or minus two, and then your brain will dig deep and go, "Uhhh…" That's your brain struggling to recall more names. After billions of dollars worth of advertising and branding, you still forget Tony the Tiger, Toucan Sam, two scoops, breakfast of champions, or that "they're magically delicious."

Try it again with brands of beer. List off as many types of beer as you can. You'll notice the same response.

How about players on your favorite team? You love that team! But you will only be able to recall seven, plus or minus two, of the players. My dad even had trouble remembering the names of his seven kids. You are wired to remember four or fewer easily, naturally, unconsciously. This is one reason why you may struggle to naturally remember all the steps in your process. When you teach a list that includes five or more steps it's not simple to memorize, remember, or learn.

Your current process

The purpose of your current process is to get to the hopeful conclusion of solving a customer's transportation needs by selling them the vehicle of their dreams. There are many variations of "The Road to the Sale" process in our industry. Your sales process may include enormous amounts of detail—guaranteed to be tough to remember, impossible to teach from desk, and make no sense at all to someone new to selling.

Your process might include some of these:

1. Meet and greet
2. Build rapport
3. Qualify the customer
4. Currently driving?
5. Pre-appraisal
6. Credit evaluation
7. Wants and needs analysis

8. Select the vehicle

9. Alternative selection

10. Walk around presentation

11. Sell it—features and benefits

12. Demo ride

13. Service introduction

14. Write-up

15. Credit application complete

16. Appraisal

17. Enter customer into relationship software

18. Payoff

19. Insurance

20. Customer proposal

21. Proposal presentation

22. Negotiate

23. Close

24. Follow-up

Whoa!!! Can a normal person remember or learn these easily? Is there anything natural about this? You've got to bury someone in redundant, boring training for it to stick. How does a manager teach this when working a deal at desk?

Why your current process is hard to learn

As a child, when you went to kindergarten or first grade, learning had to be simple. You had to be taught to learn. To help with that, you might have seen something like this in your classroom:

Aa Bb Cc Dd Ee Ff Gg Hh Ii Jj Kk Ll Mm Nn Oo Pp Qq Rr Ss Tt Uu Vv Xx Yy Zz

We are taught to learn from left to right. So why does
our industry teach the sales process from top to bottom? It
makes no sense to do things the hard way.

Twenty-six letters of the alphabet, the foundation of learning—where was it in your classroom? Did it run across the top of your chalkboard or white board? Or was it running top-to-bottom on the side of the board? *It ran across the top.*

Why was it at the top going across? Because that's how we've been taught to learn in this culture—left to right. Our whole educational system is based on learning left to right. In high school—left to right. In college—left to right. But when you become a salesperson, for some reason, we teach up and down in a list format. We expect salespeople to learn in a way they've never learned before. This is one of the reasons it's difficult to learn your process—they taught it to you top to bottom.

Let's get back to the ABCs for a moment. How in the world did you ever learn to remember 26 letters of the alphabet? That's far more than seven (plus or minus two). First of all, every letter had a picture to reinforce to the letter. A had a picture of an apple, B had a picture of a bumblebee—pictures anchored our learning. You also learned the alphabet by chunking 26 letters down into four groups and then putting the groups into a song. It went like this—

You can remember long strings of information simply by breaking it down into chunks. Just like your ABCs—you learned 26 letters in four chunks.

ABCDEFG   HIJKLMNOP   QRSTUV   WXY and Z
Now I know my ABC's...

Because there was a break after each chunk of letters, your conscious mind didn't learn the letters individually. It learned them as four pieces of a song. Whenever we have to recall where a certain letter falls in the alphabet, we will actually sing the melody in our heads. We learn and remember more when we incorporate melody. How many books do you remember all the words to? The answer is probably none, unless it was a Doctor Seuss book, which you learned because of melody. How many quotes can you remember verbatim from a book you've read and loved? Probably not very many. Now consider this: How many songs can you sing? Do you know the chorus of a song or two or three? How many melodies can you hum, if you don't sing? You'll find it's very difficult to remember text from books, but you can remember songs. Education, learning, and recall happen easily when we have fewer than five chunks together with a melody we can hook into.

How your brain processes information

So far, we've examined two reasons salespeople have trouble learning and struggle to remember the steps to the sale—there are too many steps, and they are taught up and down in a list form. The third reason we don't remember our processes is because of how our brains think.

Try this. Say or think loudly the months of the year, starting with January.

Ready, Go! January, February, _____, _____, _____, _____ ...

You will find that you'll get them all right, and you'll get through them simply and easily, unconsciously. You unconsciously know the months. Right?

Now, pay attention to how your brain works when answering this next question. Again, list the months of the year in your brain, starting with June and going backwards, stopping at July. Do this exercise. Watch how you think.

Ready, Go! June, May, _____, _____, _____, _____ ...

Different, yes? Did you get them all right? Was it easy? What was your brain picturing? Was there a list? Did you see it in a Rolodex form? Did you see it left to right, linearly? Or maybe you saw a picture of a four-by-three grid and you moved backwards that way. How was your brain processing or attempting to process the question?

Here's one more. You knew the months unconsciously in the first example. You had to think about it in the second example. Again, pay attention, be aware, and notice how your brain works in this third example. Say or think loudly the months of the year in alphabetical order. Once again, do it.

Ready, Go! April, August, _____, _____, _____, _____ ...

When you do this, you will see your brain shift and move and try to comprehend a way to piece it together. Not easy, is it? On the one hand, you know the months of the year. On the other hand, your brain has not been trained to remember them in different setups.

How we learn, think about, and remember our sales process is the key to tapping into the gold mine that this industry offers to anyone who desires wealth and happiness.

Boudreaux's Drugstore

I grew up in a drugstore. My whole life, I watched my dad and my uncle love and care for patients. If you couldn't afford your medicine, it was free. They were not attached to selling cough syrup or prescriptions. They were there to solve your health needs. They were there to help you move from not feeling well (your PROBLEM) to feeling certain you were going to become well (your POSSIBILITY). Patients would come into the drugstore, and Dad would greet them and visit with them and he would begin to ask a bunch of questions designed to GET THE PICTURE of their health. He would ask questions about how they felt and what was achy and did they have a sore throat or a temperature. When was the last time they ate?

He asked a bunch of questions all designed to GET THE PICTURE of what was going on with this person's health. In that picture, he would discover the PROBLEM and help patients move toward a POSSIBILITY. That's all Dad did, and that's all selling is. It's about curiosity, discovery, solving, and caring. Whatever you do, this is what it's all about—you get the picture?

How can you make sure your current process is easily learned, remembered, sensible, and teachable from desk?

Whatever your sales process currently is, like the alphabet, it can be chunked down into fewer steps. Three steps, actually. No matter how many steps of the sale you're currently using, you can chunk them down into this three-step, Keep It Simple process. In addition it applies to hiring new employees. It applies to service advisors, conflict resolution, and F&I people. It's about solving, and most of all, selling. The process includes three steps taught left to right; it's based on the natural behavior you've had since childhood; and it appeals to your childlike sense of curiosity and discovery. It's about solving PROBLEMS and discovering POSSIBILITIES. The process develops clarity and moves you toward closure. It works for the customer, it's easy for you, and it's 100 percent honest. So, it fits the Rules of Engagement that are so important when serving customers.

Step 1: GET THE PICTURE

The first step of your process should attempt to assess, qualify, and get an idea of what the customer is trying to accomplish. Throughout this book, we've discussed, GET THE PICTURE to discover the PP (PROBLEMS or POSSIBILITIES). What separates the salespeople who struggle from the ones that crush it? What one quality might they possess that helps them put the deals together that no one else has been able to?

They believe. *You've* got to BELIEVE.

Great salespeople believe everyone is going to buy. It doesn't matter if the customer is upside down, credit challenged, not buying today, or looking for a vehicle that's not available for two years. Successful salespeople believe.

They GET the PICTURE, discover the PP, and BELIEVE IN THE DEAL. Then they do whatever it takes to FIND THE DEAL. We talked about BS (belief systems) in chapter 5. It takes three people to believe in a deal—the customer, the manager, and you. You are the rock that always believes no matter what.

- **BELIEVE IN THE DEAL.** Every deal.
- **Believe in yourself.** Who you are, at your best. And think, "I'm going to treat everyone like royalty."
- **Believe in your product.** You've got to know you sell the best product and that it's going to solve the customer's transportation needs. It's going to heal them, cure them, get rid of their Problems, or give them the Possibility of having the feeling they're looking for.
- **Believe in your dealership.** Find a dealer who fits your values and stay there! "At this dealership, we bust our butts for our customers; the customer comes first." That's the kind of place you want to be associated with.
- **Believe in your relationships.** You're responsible for the relationships. You're responsible for being present, for being respectful, and for being likable.
- **Believe in your brand.** You've got to know your manufacturer stands behind the car you're selling. I've been in this industry since 1983, and it's been an honor and a pleasure to work with the greatest partners in the world—the manufacturers who build our products!

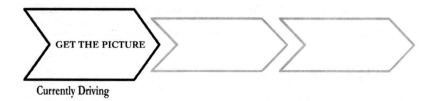

Currently Driving

One of the first things you can do to GET THE PICTURE is ask questions about what the customer is currently driving.

Specifically, you can ask questions like—

- What are you currently driving?
- Did you buy it new or previously enjoyed?
- When did you buy it?
- When is your next payment due?
- How much do you pay per month?
- Really, how did you get your payments so low?
- What do you like most about it? What else do you like? What else?
- What don't you like? What else don't you like? What else?

Auto industry expert, Grant Cardone, has been teaching these questions for years now, and with good reason. These are great questions to Get the Picture and discover the PP.

How did they purchase this vehicle? When? Why? Problems. Possibilities. Values. Expectations. Equipment. Money. You can discover a lot of information just by asking great questions. Every question gives you a better picture.

"When's your next payment due?" You might discover that they're late on payments, or early, or maybe it's about to come due, so they could use that money towards the down payment.

"What do you like most about what you're currently driving?" (What else? What else?) This is a great question to discover the POSSIBILITIES, and what the customer values in the current vehicle that is important and that he or she may want in the next vehicle.

"What *don't* you like about your current vehicle?" (What else? What else?) Discover the PROBLEMS they're moving away from. Maybe they don't like the gas mileage, or the fact that it was in a wreck two weeks ago and has a strange sound coming from the engine. Or maybe it belonged to her ex-husband and she can't stand being in it another day. There are things they don't like about this vehicle; it's your job to find them out. Get the Picture, so far?

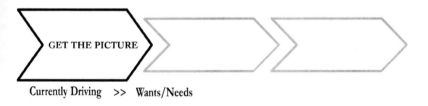

GET THE PICTURE

Currently Driving   >>   Wants/Needs

Next discover their WANTS, NEEDS and USE of their next vehicle. Some questions to discover what they WANT and NEED are:

- Car, truck, or SUV?
- Cloth or leather? Light, medium, or darker colors?
- Automatic or standard?
- Sunroof? Heated seats? Power seats? Tow package?
- Two-wheel drive or four-wheel?
- Which trim package?
- Stereo system?

Some questions to discover how they USE the vehicle:

- Who else drives the vehicle?
- Who else rides in the vehicle? Kids? Spouse? Critters?
- Do you take any special trips?
- Do you pull a trailer with the vehicle?
- Do you have a specific hobby you need the vehicle for?

All these questions continue to help GET THE PICTURE so that the salesperson can narrow down the choices and direct the customer to the lowest-priced, in-stock unit that fits the picture.

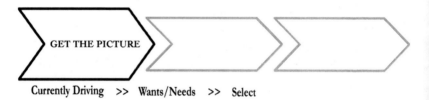

Currently Driving   >>   Wants/Needs   >>   Select

Select a vehicle. Ever had a customer who says, "I want the red one, I want the red one!"? You walk up to the red one, and then she says, "Not that red one, the other shade of red." Showing customers an in-stock vehicle is critical when Getting Their Picture.

Sell from stock. Have you ever had a month selling where you were in "the zone"; everybody wanted to buy from you? It was *your* month! Remember that? Guaranteed, you weren't doing a lot of dealer trades. There's nothing that pulls you out of the zone faster than trying to find a bunch of vehicles from other dealers who aren't willing to give up great inventory. Why is it that some salespeople can sell 40 to 60 cars a month and rarely do dealer trades, while other salespeople only sell 12 cars, and half of them are dealer trades?

It's very simple. Salespeople are taught to ask questions and GET THE PICTURE. Then they typically say, "Based on this picture, these are the three vehicles my brand makes that will work best for you."

But that's not what great salespeople do. Great salespeople ask more questions, get a better picture, understand the PP (Problems and Possibilities), and say, "Based on what's *available*, this is the vehicle that will work best for you." And then they take the customer right to that vehicle. To sell more vehicles from stock: ask questions, GET THE PICTURE, and show the customer the lowest priced, in stock unit that fits their picture.

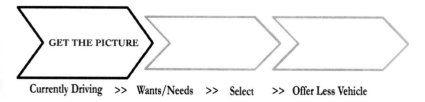

Currently Driving >> Wants/Needs >> Select >> Offer Less Vehicle

Offer a less expensive vehicle to get the money picture early. Another part of selecting the right vehicle for the customer is money. Grant Cardone called this step "alternative selection"— brilliant. Here's why you want to find out if money is an issue early in the deal and not when you're trying to close. Ask the customer, "Would you like to save a little money by getting something with less equipment?" Offer a less expensive trim level. Offer a less expensive model. Maybe he'd like to save some money by going to a previously enjoyed car.

For example, you might say, "Before I show you this vehicle, would you consider a similar one that doesn't have the leather seats, the navigation, or the sunroof? That will lower your price about $4,000 and drop your payment maybe as much as $80 a month. Would you like that one instead?"

The customer might say yes or he might say no. Part of GET THE PICTURE is offering a less expensive vehicle, less equipment, a trim level down, or a different model. You are putting a floor in the negotiation for later. You're getting the picture of how low they are willing to go. All of these questions are part of Get the Picture to discover the PP.

When you understand the customer's PP, you can use those Problems and Possibilities as leverage to make it easier for the customer to buy now. Most salespeople try to influence the customer by dropping the payment $20 to get them to buy. I ask salespeople how much it costs them to drop the payment by $20. Invariably, they say it costs them $1,000. That's not true. It costs the dealer $1,000. It costs *them* whatever their commissionable amount is of that $1,000. It could be as much as $200 to $300 in some cases. Every time you go to the desk and the manager drops $40, it costs you more commissionable gross based on that $2,000 drop. Great salespeople aren't using $20 to influence the customer; they're using the Problem or the Possibility as leverage to help that customer buy now.

Customers will say, "I want the red one," and if you don't have a red one, they use that to stall, negotiate, or put off buying from you. Why are there salespeople who rarely miss a deal because of color—and others who seem to struggle with this often? It's because of the PP. Most of the time, unless it's a really high-end luxury car, it's not about "red." It's something much deeper that will get them to move forward now. It's about "help me move away from this car that has a noise in the engine" or "help me move toward this vehicle that will make me look more successful to my friends."

Before you move on to the second step in the process, make sure you have their PP! You're going to need it all the way through to the close

Second grade selling. The greatest salespeople and closers are currently in second and third grades. They are bold, fearless, tenacious, certain, urgent, energetic, enthusiastic, happy, flexible, resourceful, persistent, expressive, compelling, curious, funny, emotional, present, optimistic, driven, and determined. They get what they want.

And when they don't get the outcome they desire, what do they do? They turn to their little brother, sister, cousin, or friend and whisper, "YOU ask him; he'll say yes to you!" In the auto industry, we call that a T.O. (turn over). You think that's funny? Consider this, when those kids still don't get the outcome they desire, do they give up? No! They immediately go ask a different manager— mom—fully expecting to get the correct outcome. Second graders know that you have to try many different approaches to accomplish your goal.

In the auto industry, the purpose of the T.O. is not to sell a car. The purpose is to progress the conversation to the next step. If you're in the beginning stages—the Get The Picture process—and the customer won't let you do a walk-around or a product presentation or let you demo the car or go to a write up, then you want to get a manager involved. T.O. the customer so that the sales manager can move the sale to the next step. Remember, the goal always is to solve the customer's Problem or Possibility. The benefit of the T.O. is for the customer. The customer benefits because someone else came in to solve their Problem or Possibility. You weren't able to solve it, but maybe a set of fresh questions, fresh ears, fresh perspective, or different person will make it easier—so you can still accomplish the goal of solving the customer's transportation needs.

Second graders are brilliant, because they utilize everything at their disposal to solve their problem or realize what's possible for themselves. A second grader's mission statement is clear. A second grader says, "I am _____, _____, and _____ so I can get Mom and Dad to say *yes!*" New salespeople and great salespeople do this naturally.

Step 2: GIVE INFO

Give information that fits the picture. After you GET THE PICTURE, you move to the second step in the Keep It Simple process. In your process, these might include steps number four, eight, or even ten. The goal here is to be interesting, entertaining, and fun. This is Disneyland. It's show time. Get the customer excited about this vehicle that's going to fit his picture and solve his PP perfectly!

Remember, you're going to give information *based on the picture you got in step one.* You're not going to verbally vomit 30,000 pounds of information or everything you know about a Toyota truck. You're going to focus on what's *relevant* to this customer. Give information based on the picture.

If a lady had a wreck and totaled her van with her three children inside, and she's concerned about safety, then focus on and GIVE INFO based on safety, security, and peace of mind. On the other hand, if she just got divorced, her children have all grown and left the nest, and she's wanting to be sporty, adventurous, and fast—then you're going to want to GIVE INFO showing her how your vehicle will give her that sleek, sexy, and fun feeling she desires. It's all based on the picture you got in the first step. Get The Picture?

Here are three activities that fall under the Give Info step—the product presentation, the demo ride, and the service walk or introduction.

Product Presentation

Product presentation. Start on the outside, and then move to the inside. In the product presentation you show the customers what they're getting for their money. You want to provide compelling information that shows them how the vehicles you are presenting will help them solve their PP. The purpose here is to build more value than price. When done correctly, this step puts them into a position where they must move to this outstanding, incredible vehicle regardless of the price.

The way you accomplish that is by providing the customer with an incredibly powerful product presentation where you show them all the features and benefits that fit their picture. Now, features and benefits can be confusing. So, let me make it simple for you.

"Features and benefits" in its simplest form:

Feature: Here's the physical thing you're showing them.

Benefit: And here's what's so great about it.

That's all there is to it.

Brakes. And here's what's so great about them.

Wheels. And here's what's so great about them.

This special transmission. Here's what's so great about it.

This navigation system. Here's what's so great about it.

Now let's kick it up a notch. Anyone can run through features and benefits. It's pretty standard, and often a little boring. But here's how you can immediately improve your product presentation: use Features, Benefits, and Distinction. This is where you build real value and make money.

Distinction is simply adding "and this is what's so great about OURS" to the standard features and benefits statements.

Here's what Features/Benefits/Distinction looks like:

This car has _____ (Feature) *so that* _____, _____, and _____ (Benefits). And _____ is why OURS is the best (Distinction).

This car has ABS brakes. So that you can stop safely even in treacherous conditions, and our ABS brakes also (do, help, achieve) _____, _____, and _____.

Features, Benefits, and Distinction allow you to be outstanding in the marketplace compared to the salesperson that the customer spoke to earlier (or will speak to tomorrow). After all, it's your job to look much better than the person they spoke to at the other dealership. You want to beat the competition to a demoralized, fearful pulp, and eliminate them. When you use Feature/Benefit/Distinction to reinforce how your product fits the customer's Picture and solves their PP, your profitability will improve. This is what I prided myself on—my product presentation. I wanted to do it better than anyone else in the business. And in my opinion, I did.

Product knowledge. New salespeople are paralyzed with fear because they don't think they know enough about the vehicle that a customer might desire. How do you shorten the learning curve? How do you figure out all that technical stuff that keeps you from being confident in your ability to help someone? Is there a shortcut?

New people, do this: Pick out the vehicle you LOVE the most on the lot. Grab a full-sized notebook of some sort and write down EVERYTHING you see, like, or notice about the vehicle. Touch everywhere. Write about the lines, the aerodynamics, the color, and the way it would look in your driveway.

Open the hood. Be aware of everything you see. Notice how the engine looks. Turn on the engine and write down how it sounds, and how it feels. Look at the wheels and tires on the passenger side of the car…keep writing. Open and close the front door. Turn the stereo on inside the vehicle, and then open and close the door. Check out the gas cap, and imagine pulling into the station. Look at the back end, notice the lights, have someone turn on the blinkers, press the brakes and emergency flashers. Open the trunk…now climb on in. I'm serious, climb in…laugh cause you'll remember that. Keep writing. Where's the spare tire? Take it out. Open the back door, climb in, and shut the door. Notice, touch, and experience everything in the backseat. You are writing all this down, aren't you?

Get in the driver's seat; don't those seats feel perfect? Now the fun begins. Look at the door and all the buttons…*touch*. Touch and operate every one of them. Feel the air from the side window defroster. Adjust your mirrors. Keep going. Oh yeah, BREATHE IN…smell the *new*. Folks in the business have lost that smell; it's there though. Write about it; always remember the power of your sense of smell. Look at the way the speedometer, gauges, lights on the dash, and indicator light look and feel. Check out the navigation system, program in the location of the dealership and your favorite restaurant. Look at the center console, glove box, storage compartments, and pockets. Put your hand inside all of them. Smile; it gets better. TAKE OFF. Go for a ride. Fast, slow, brakes, ride, turning radius, power, visibility—pull over and write it all down.

After you have written pages of amazing, fun, exciting, emotional, crazy notes about what you love most about the vehicle, then go watch the training video. When you learn to talk about what you love from your heart, the customer will feel it. Your passion will shine through. Love one car, and you'll have a framework for every car you ever need to sell. Get The Picture?

Product Presentation   >>   Demo Ride

The demo ride. Before you take a demo ride, you want your customers to be completely at ease. They should be comfortable with the vehicle inside and out. Take some time to help them learn the inside of the car. Let them climb in on the passenger's side; you sit in the driver's seat so you can give them a tour of the inside.

Use sensory words like *touch this*, *notice this*, *smell that*, and *imagine this*.

Have them touch the fabric or leather. If you have leather seats, you show them how soft, supple, and buttery they feel. Tell them, "This leather doesn't have a heavy vinyl topcoat," so they won't get that burning sensation on their legs when it's in the hot sun.

Show them how to work the power windows, power locks, how to roll the windows up and down.

Show them the rearview mirrors and how they move.

Show them the side defogger.

Show them how much room they can see around them—all the visibility in the world.

Talk about the ergonomics and cockpit design and all the different instruments.

Make sure they know how everything works. Talk about the gas gauge, where the button is to release the gas cap, and which side to fill up the car.

Then move to the air conditioning system. Tell them how it takes out all the lint, dust, and pollen. Tell them how it's environmentally safe.

You'll also want to tell them about the stereo system—whatever flavor stereo it is. Tell them about everything—and let them get the feel of it. Customers are comfortable with playing with the sound system. So step aside and let them have fun.

Talk about the transmission and how it shifts.

Show them how to adjust the seat belt. In fact, put yours on and have them put theirs on and adjust it so it fits them. Then, you adjust the driver's side seatbelt to fit them, so that when they get in to drive, it fits them perfectly.

Once they get into the driver's seat, let the demo ride last somewhere between 30 and 40 minutes. Don't rush this step! The longer the demo ride, the more spiritually connected they get to the car. Here's why the longer the demo ride, the better off the customer is. The first 10 or 15 minutes of the ride, they're thinking *touch this, feel this, imagine this, I wonder how much it's going to cost, I'm not sure how good my credit is, I'm not buying this today, I hope I can make something work...* They're in their heads, thinking about all the different reasons why this shouldn't happen today. They are consciously doing battle with the logic of this decision.

At some point, they will drift off and move to their imagination. They are driving somewhere else. They are seeing themselves pull into their favorite bar or the valet parking at their favorite restaurant. They imagine pulling up to work where their co-workers are checking out their new truck. They're feeling proud. *You want this feeling to linger.*

Another reason you want to take a longer demo ride is that noise. You know, *that* noise. How many of you have had a noise in your car? A squeak or rattle or a noise when you made a turn, and you just knew your wheel was going to fall off. You were sure everybody could hear this embarrassing noise. Your customer has that noise, too. They may not even realize how bad that noise is until they get in a vehicle that doesn't have it. Your car does not have that noise. Your car is humming. It's telling them, "Buy me, cause I like you, too." Don't interrupt them.

The longer you drive, the more they drift off and imagine owning this vehicle. Stop talking, and let them enjoy it.

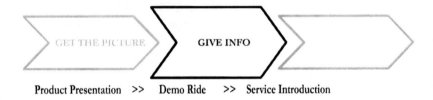

GET THE PICTURE > GIVE INFO

Product Presentation   >>   Demo Ride   >>   Service Introduction

Service introduction. When you get back into your dealership, pull into the service lane if it's not too busy. You want to introduce your customer to a service advisor or manager. This is the third step of GIVE INFO—doing a service walk or introduction. This is where you're going to have your service advisor or manager talk to the customer.

They're going to say, "Congratulations! You're going to love that new car. I want to give you a little brochure that shows you our service hours. It tells you about the service department, and what we do for you when you come in. We have a great service lounge with delicious beverages. We also have a shuttle that will take you to work or the mall or the movie theater. And I'm going to take care of your first oil change." Let the service advisor offer the complimentary first oil change. That's how you build a lifelong relationship and build value at this point. Show the customer how friendly and helpful everyone at the dealership is.

Toyota Motor Corporation says that 60 percent of the people who visit a dealership's service department three times will buy again from that dealership. You want to encourage the customer to come back over and over again. (And then *you* want to STAY at that dealership, because the customer is creating loyalty with you *at that dealership*.)

Be sure to introduce the customer to the service department, and have one of the service advisors sell how great the service department is. After you GIVE INFO that fits the customer's picture, simply say, "Come on inside, and I'll show you how easy it is to do business with us!"

Step 3: OFFER SOLUTIONS WITH CHOICES

Solve the PP: Offer solutions with choices—The Close. If GET THE PICTURE is about *discovering* the PP, then OFFERING SOLUTIONS WITH CHOICES is about *solving* the PP. This is about offering different payments OR plans so the customer has a choice between "yes" and "yes," not "yes" or "no." Instead of deciding to go someplace else, they are saying, "I can choose something close."

You want to set up the close early in the deal. Have the right car for the customer's picture—the one that's *in stock* and matches their PP the best. You're going to want to find out what's more important: budget or vehicle. You ask questions to Get The Picture and discover the PP. You take the customer to the lowest price, in-stock unit that fits his or her picture. Remember earlier when I told you it was important to help the customer save money by offering less vehicle early on? Well, now is when that pre-framing comes in handy.

Let's review that step for just a moment:

Say the in-stock vehicle that fits the customer's picture best is a base model Explorer. What might you say to save them some money?

"Would you consider a nicer-equipped Edge? It will save you about $4,000 or $5,000. That's about $80 to $100 dollars per month if you go from an Explorer to an Edge."

Let's assume that the customer says, "No. I don't want the Edge. I want that Explorer." What you've done is put a floor into the negotiation. And you've done it early, well before you ever talk about price or payments.

If the customer is looking at a top-of-the-line, fully-loaded Explorer, you might ask, "Would you consider an Explorer that doesn't have the sunroof, navigation system, or the heated leather seats? It's about a $4,000 drop in price. That's about $80 a month in savings. Do you want the nicer one, or the one with less equipment?"

Chances are, the customer will probably say, "The nicer one."

Again, we have a floor in the price. That customer has already said they don't want the less expensive model. So, when it comes time for the close, and that customer says the price is too high, where do you go from there? You go back to that lower-model or lesser-equipped vehicle. The customer put that floor into the negotiation *before* hearing the price of the desired vehicle. The customer's subconscious is going to resist settling for that lesser vehicle because they already stated they didn't want it.

Write Up

Transition to write-up. You want to do a write-up on every customer. Everybody gets a price. It doesn't matter if they plan to buy today or not buy today. It doesn't matter if they're upside down, credit challenged, or they're waiting for a model that's not even designed yet—*it doesn't matter.* If we treat people like shoppers, they will shop. When we believe people are buyers, they will buy. You've got to believe in the deal. Don't be concerned if they go somewhere else. Be *so confident* in yourself, your dealership, your pricing, and your product that your customers would be absolute fools not to let *you* solve their Problems or move toward new Possibilities.

Write Up   >>   CRM

Grow your relationship tree. You want to enter *everybody* into your customer relationship management (CRM) database. This is your apple tree. It's where you build relationships for life. Enter all prospects—their names, addresses, all phone numbers, email, what they're currently driving, where they saw the advertisement. (If lots of people saw ads in the Thrifty Nickel, guess where I'm going to start advertising as a salesperson?). Most importantly, keep track of any ongoing conversations you've been having with them. What kind of business do they own? Are they expecting a new baby? That might be a reason to follow up with them later on to say "congratulations." Recurring conversations gets you recurring revenue.

Prepare the paperwork. Next, get *all* your paperwork ready to bring to the desk. If you have trouble keeping track of paperwork when you're selling 12 vehicles, try keeping track when you're selling 40. You have to start treating paperwork like you're selling 40. I am not an organized person. So, I started filling out *all* the paperwork before I touched the desk. I had to. It was the only way to keep everything straight, and it helped me so much. Full credit apps, all the stips, verified insurance, payoff, and copies of their driver's license—everything was done so that when I touched desk, it was all there. Then, when it was time to close, I could just say, "Circle the option that works best for you." Once the customer circled it, I didn't have to do any more paperwork before I went to F&I.

Then all that was left to do was say, "Congratulations! You're going to love your new truck!"

Start all deals at full price and shorter terms. You want to start all deals at full price, whatever that is for your store. Shorter terms, higher down payments, and reduced ACV (actual cash value)— it's scary, for some. The biggest fear around doing this is that the customer will blow out and you'll lose the deal. You may be afraid they will physically stand up and walk away. But in reality, less than five percent of customers will ever stand up. Most salespeople structure their deals based on what *might* happen about five percent of the time. Of that five percent, only two to three percent will actually walk out without negotiating. You stay seated. This will work out fine. Really. The first few times you do this, it may freak you out a little; enjoy the feeling.

Ideally, you want 36 to 48-month terms. Why do you want shorter terms? Seventy-two months is a long time. You want that customer for life, right? You want a great relationship with that customer, right? Well, how do you think they're going to feel 48 months into a 72 month contract? They're going to feel trapped. They're going to feel like you stuck them with a vehicle they never liked—even if they did like it at first. After that much time goes by, they are starting to think about getting a new vehicle, but they're trapped in a long-term payment plan. On the other hand, if they have shorter terms, they're going to come back to you excited about what you've got waiting for them next. *Lifelong relationships.*

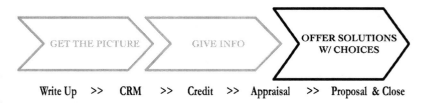

Proposal presentation and closing the deal. The next part of Offering Solutions With Choices is to go see the customer, give a proposal presentation, and close the sale. The purpose of the proposal presentation is to let the prospect choose the payment, down payment, or term that works best for them. If something doesn't fit, then offer the non-discount closes to show the customer how to afford *this* selection, or to show them how to afford another selection *without* discounting your price.

Non-discount closes are what I call "offensive plays." They are set up so you do not give away your gross. The gross you start at is where you want to end up. When you can get the customer to agree, and they feel like they negotiated, then you will maximize your profits.

Not everyone feels comfortable with the fancy closes. I want to make it simple and natural, so you can just do the same thing over and over again. These closes use body language and high-level communication skills. Once you see them, you're going to want to change them so that they fit how you talk, think, and feel. Make them yours!

Training you to use non-discount closes is an entire video course in itself. My project manager wanted me to keep it as a product for sale. But I want you to have it as a bonus gift, as a reward for getting this far through the book. Congratulations! You need to see this in a video format; you won't get it if you just read it. So here's what you should do…

I want you to go to <u>www.autotrainingacademy.com/non-discount-closes/</u> and watch the video there. Do this as soon as you can. Don't skip it!

All of my closes are respectful, simple, and don't make you look or feel uncomfortable. You're going to love them. Go watch the video.

So what are the steps for KEEP IT SIMPLE SELLING again? As you can see, all I've done is take your current multi-step process and chunked it down into three steps: Get the Picture, Give Information, and Offer Solutions With Choices. These three steps are part of your natural behavior, and you can chunk the steps of every dealer process down to them.

You Get The Picture?

Teaching at desk

A good sales process is one that's easy to remember, based on natural behavior, and is *teachable at desk*. There's a huge disconnect in this industry between learning and teaching, between what we teach and what we do. All too often, teaching is done in a classroom, separate from the actual sales floor. Once those salespeople go back to the lot, they're left to their own shortcomings and uncertainty. The skills they learn online are rarely reinforced, which means there's only a small chance they'll get used at all. Teaching needs to be easier and more duplicatable, and it needs to match what we're asking the salesperson to do.

Managers, I'm talking to you right now. Teaching at desk should happen every time a newer salesperson (or someone who's struggling) comes to the desk. When salespeople come to the desk, you want to be glad to see them! Show them you're excited about working deals with them. Reassure them that you're going to help them out. And model the same three steps you're asking them to follow in the Keep It Simple process.

Teach salespeople how to Get The Picture and to share the PP with the desk! Every salesperson who comes to see you needs to *bring you the picture* they got from the customer. They need to share the PP with you so that you can prepare a proposal that fits the picture. You can help this along if every manager in your store asks the same six to ten questions of every person who comes to desk. You're hoping the salesperson has the answers so that you can get the correct picture.

Here are some questions you could ask the salesperson:

- What is this customer currently driving?
- How long has he/she had it?
- Where did he/she finance it?
- When's his/her next payment due?
- How much is his/her next payment?
- How'd he/she get the payment so low?
- What does he/she like most about the car? What else? What else?
- What doesn't he/she like about it? What else? What else?
- What lesser-equipped vehicle did you offer him/her on the lot to save money?
- Did he/she like the way the vehicle drove?

The salesperson's job is to answer these questions and share the picture with you. This way, you have a clear picture so that you can put together a profitable proposal.

Now, if a salesperson comes to the desk and does NOT have the picture, you'll want to get up and go GET THE PICTURE yourself! Show the salesperson how to do it properly. If you don't make absolutely sure you have the picture, you may be on the wrong car. You might have a vehicle in stock that's better suited to fit this person's picture. That customer may be on a vehicle that isn't in stock, which means you'll need to do a dealer trade when you could offer them the recently traded for, previously enjoyed, in-stock vehicle that you can deliver today. You have the ability to help the salesperson to increase sales based on your expertise at Getting The Picture and discovering the PP. After you have the picture and everything you need from the salesperson, have the salesperson go back to the customer to build and maintain the relationship. There is no need for the salesperson to wait around the desk while you are structuring the deal and preparing the proposal worksheet. The salesperson can connect with you when the deal is ready to present. That's the first step. Get The Picture?

GET THE PICTURE   GIVE INFO

GIVE INFO to teach strategies and **CREATE CERTAINTY.** Remember, when preparing your proposal, you want to start all deals at full price, with shorter terms and reduced ACV and higher down payments. Everyone collects more money that way. Some salespeople will be nervous when they first try this. Their fears are very real. They truly believe that the customers will blow out if they don't get the best deal every time. There are salespeople in every dealership who say, "I've got one shot at this. We have to give them our best price, or they're going to leave." They believe it. There's not a doubt in their minds it's going to happen. They can feel the opportunity slipping away before they even get to your office. It's unconscious. These salespeople might be in survival mode; they're hungry for a paycheck, and they just want to make a deal. They believe that if they offer the best deal every time, they will make more money.

Managers, when this happens, you have to get up out of your chairs and go make the deal. *You* have to show the salesperson it's going to be okay. You have to physically get up and go talk to the customer. Show them the higher numbers, and let the salesperson see it's okay; you're going to work it out. You might have to do this three or four times, but eventually they will understand and be able to present the higher numbers themselves.

When you're giving information, your goal is to teach strategies that give and instill complete certainty so that the salesperson can confidently close the deal. When they go to sit down with the customer, it's a done deal in the salesperson's head. You don't want to have a salesperson walking away from the sales desk uncertain, doubtful, or fearful about the next conversation they'll have with the customer. You want the salesperson to feel 10 feet tall and invincible and ready to conquer the world. Managers are taught to load the salesperson's lips. I want you to load their whole body! Put your salespeople in positions of strength, power, and certainty—so they know they can go in with strategies that work for the customers, that work for them, and that are 100 percent honest. Your job is to give the salespeople information that lets them easily and naturally offer solutions with choices.

This is how simple this process is. It works for salespeople. It helps managers teach. It works for the customers. It's 100 percent honest. That's what I'm selling. Keep It Simple is all about *solving*; it's about *serving*; and best of all, it's about *selling*—in a simple, yet effective way.

Own it!

Okay, time to implement what you've learned in this chapter. First things first. Go watch the *Non-Discount Closes* training online. You'll find it at http://autotrainingacademy.com/non-discount-closes/

Fill in the blanks below with words from your I AM list.

What qualities, characteristics, and values must I have so that I can Get The Picture while I am with a customer? Write your list, and then narrow it down to what will drive you.

I am _____   I am _____

I am _____   I am _____

I am _____   I am _____

I am _____   I am _____

I am _____   I am _____

I am _____   I am _____

I am _____   I am _____

I am _____, _____, and _____ so that _____.

What qualities, characteristics, and values must I have so that I can give the best product presentation in the business? Write your list, and then narrow it down to what will drive you.

I am _____   I am _____

I am _____   I am _____

I am _____   I am _____

I am _____   I am _____

I am _____   I am _____

I am _____   I am _____

I am _____, _____, and _____ so that _____.

What qualities, characteristics, and values must I have so that I can solve the customer's PP while being profitable and proud of what I do? Write your list, and then narrow it down to what will drive you.

I am _____	I am _____
I am _____	I am _____
I am _____	I am _____
I am _____	I am _____
I am _____	I am _____
I am _____	I am _____
I am _____	I am _____

I am _____, _____, and _____ so that _____.

What qualities, characteristics, and values must I have so that I am driven, ambitious, and an unstoppable force in my profession? Write your list, and then narrow it down to what will drive you.

I am _____	I am _____
I am _____	I am _____
I am _____	I am _____
I am _____	I am _____
I am _____	I am _____
I am _____	I am _____
I am _____	I am _____

I am _____, _____, and _____ so that _____.

BREAK THE RULES...WRITE IN THE BOOK!

_____
_____
_____
_____
_____
_____
_____
_____
_____
_____
_____
_____
_____
_____
_____
_____
_____
_____
_____
_____
_____
_____
_____
_____
_____
_____

Chapter Eight

LEADERSHIP

"Great leaders lead themselves first."

T his business is a gold mine. You've heard me tell you all sorts of success stories—like the guy who started washing cars and ended up as the general manager. This happened because of great leadership. Many leaders in our industry are looked up to, held up, and admired as great examples of what's possible for people just getting into the business. Whether you wash cars or answer phones, this business is your gold mine. Great managers and leaders can help you understand who you are at your best, and teach you how to serve and care for others. This is what great leaders do—raise people up, nurture them, and help them grow.

Other managers and leaders, on the other hand, create anger, animosity, distrust, and contribute to a terrible reputation for our industry. Managers get fired exponentially more often than salespeople. They get fired by upper management for lack of performance or behavior, and they also get fired by salespeople and employees when they quit as a direct result of management not teaching, appreciating, supporting, or caring about them. You want to be part of a winning team led by a winning coach.

So, how do you become that great leader, coach, mentor, and role model? How do you teach in a way that's inspirational, simple, natural, and duplicatable? That's what this chapter is all about. You might be wondering why I wrote this chapter, when most of this book is for salespeople? I was a salesperson, and you are the ones I want to help. So, I'm including this chapter for you, because one day you may be a manager, a GM, or an owner. And I want you to be able to succeed at that level and share this gold mine with others. I want you to surpass all your peers and create massive abundance for yourself and for everyone who works with you. I want you to dominate your market. And guess what? Everything you've learned so far will help you do that. All you have to do is look at it from a slightly different angle—the way you wish you could have been taught by your managers. Not just the great one, but all of them.

I want to make this great industry even better for the people who work in it. I want people in every department to experience massive success. Managers are hungry to be great coaches and mentors. But they need more tools and strategies. Most are where they are because they were great salespeople. They teach the same way they were taught, which in some cases was: *I'm going to beat you into a demoralized pulp until you get it. And the beatings will continue until the attitude improves.* Okay, not everyone is like that, and the industry has improved in recent years. Let's make it even better.

Your investment portfolio

David Bach wrote the book *Automatic Millionaire*. I highly recommend you read it. In this book, he says accumulating wealth isn't so much about what you make; it's about how much you don't spend. What we're trained to do in this society is to go to work and collect money every month, and then most people invest their collected money into liabilities. Your house, car, utility bills, credit cards, cell phone, children's activities, entertainment, restaurants—these are your liabilities. Then they save what little is left over (if anything).

David says *save money first*. Then pay your liabilities—so you can take your savings and invest it in profit centers like stocks, bonds, real estate, etc. Once you're investing in profit centers, the dividends from those investments can pay for your liabilities. Investments are great things. They can bring you money for the rest of your life, if you manage them properly. If you research them, invest in the good ones, and nurture them; weed out the bad ones, and help the good ones grow. You'll have a great portfolio that you are proud of and that grows and builds your wealth.

Guess what?

Salespeople are a manager's retirement portfolio—Invest in them!

When I was a new salesman, maybe three or four months into selling cars, I remember getting a call to come to Mr. Red Hickman's office.

Mr. Red was the general manager of the dealership; and when I went in there, I just knew I was in trouble. It felt like I was going to the principal's office at school again. Well, I went in, and he asked me to sit down. And I did, nervously.

"Boudreaux, do you remember the other day when we were talking to a customer together, and he had a big gold chain on his wrist? Do you remember that?"

"Yes, sir!" I said, "That was a really nice chain. I've been wanting a chain like that my whole life."

"Well, I was at the jewelry store the other day, and I looked down and saw this." He opened up his drawer and pulled out a very expensive looking box. He opened it up, and I saw a gold chain. "Is this what you were hoping for?"

My eyes popped open wide and I said, "Oh, yes! That's beautiful. Isn't that a good looking chain?"

He said, "Yes it is. Why don't you try it on?" and he draped it over my wrist. And I looked at it on my wrist and admired how nice it looked sitting there. "Do you like this chain?" he asked.

"I sure do," I answered as I handed it back to him.

Then Mr. Red said something else as he carefully put it back in the box. "Damian, I know you like that chain. I want you to have it. But I have to get you to make some real money. Here's what I'm going to do. If you sell 11 cars for me this month, I will give you this gold chain." Now, I had been struggling to sell seven or eight cars, so 11 seemed like a lot to me then. But Mr. Red believed in me. He said, "Anytime customers say they don't want to buy a car, you bring them in to see me. I want to talk to them. You can do this. I believe in you. Nothing would make me happier this month than to give you this gold chain."

Let me tell you, I went to work! I talked to people everywhere. I was driven, because I wanted that gold chain. And at the end of the month, I got it. I wore that chain with pride because it stood for my success and accomplishment.

What's their gold chain?

The point of the story isn't about my taste in jewelry. I want you to see that it's important to understand what motivates your employees to do better. What's their gold chain? Mr. Red saw the good in me. He knew there was more right in me than wrong. He saw me at my best, and decided he was going to nurture the good. He was going to help me be successful. That man helped me be better than I ever dreamed I could be, all because he knew what I wanted and what would motivate me. Are you doing that? Do you know your employees well enough to find the exact thing that will motivate *them?* Is it a trip? Is it jewelry? Is it family time? Is it a management position? Or is it just a kind word and attention from you? Whatever it is, you need to know. And you need to use their gold chains as leverage to help them work harder and achieve more than they dream they can.

This is how you develop your profit centers. Invest in your employees and everyone wins. You have to help them grow. Mr. Red challenged me to do my job better. He taught me and then empowered me to get what I wanted. He tracked my progress and told me, "You're almost there, Boudreaux. You can do it!" He put me in the position where I had to succeed.

Are you challenging your people? Are you inspiring them? Do you tell them you believe in them—with your actions as well as your words? As a leader, your job is to discover their gold chains, and then leverage them. Take pride in their success. Be a teacher. Be a mentor.

Be a role model and coach. At some point, you have to ask yourself if you want to build and grow your people, or whether you're going to continue to rely on hopeium to be successful. Remember, the business of your business is people. And the key to massive success is to build and maintain incredible employees, so you can be profitable and proud of what you do. Hiring to retire means finding and leading people so they are successful for the long term.

How to hire the right people

Management is responsible for the energy, the environment, and the experience of the dealership. Culture begins at the top. If you've hired 100 people and you still don't have the right people, the people aren't the problem!

When you have an employee who fits your values and belongs at your dealership and they're not doing a good job, that's your fault. You're doing something wrong as a leader. But being a good leader starts way before that point. It starts in the hiring process. Most people hire or recruit anyone who's breathing. Don't do that! Hire good people who fit your values and are passionate about something, so they can be even more successful than you are.

How do you know if potential employees fit in your organization? Go back to the KISS process. Ask questions—you know, to Get The Picture. Discover their PP. Are they moving away from a Problem like a bankruptcy or a bad marriage? Or are they moving toward the Possibility of earning great money for the first time in their lives? Ask questions to Get The Picture of who you're hiring. Recruit people all the time, but look for certain qualities and characteristics, and only hire the ones that fit your values.

A simple strategy for hiring the right people is:

- Three interviews
- Three people
- Three different locations

I want different people in the organization coming together and agreeing that "She's our girl! She is the one we can invest in. We can pour our hearts and souls into mentoring her, and it will pay off in spades!" When three people hold three different interviews in three different places, they're going to see three different things in this woman. And they're all valid.

The first way you Get The Picture is to get three different views of her resume. That gives you a nice snapshot. If you like the picture so far, then you can invite her in for the interview. The goal of the interview process is for you to ask challenging questions—you know, to Get The Picture. You want to discover drive. Is this person driven by something. Is she passionate about something? I like to ask, "What do you love to do?"

Do your recruits like to cook? Or maybe they're passionate about their families or where they're from or they like cars or sports, music or gardening. It doesn't matter what they're passionate about, only that they are passionate about *something*.

Be present in the interview. Get rid of the distractions and focus on that person. She deserves your attention. Ask follow-up questions like, "What's your favorite thing to cook?" or "Who's your favorite quarterback?" And pay attention to how she communicates. Is she passionate? Does she raise her volume, pitch, and speed when she talks about what she does for fun? Or does she speak in a monotone voice? Can you feel the enthusiasm and excitement when she talks? If not, she probably won't have any enthusiasm when she's selling your cars, either. Does she lean in when she's talking; does she use body language; does her breathing increase? Pay attention to what's going on with her communication style. You can teach her how to sell cars. But you cannot teach passion, desire, or drive. It has to be present to start with.

You also want to ask other questions to discover the PP:

- What are the Problems and Possibilities in her life?
- What does she dream of achieving?
- What is her greatest belief system? Does she have a scarcity mindset, or does she say, "I got this! I want this!"
- What are her past experiences at work?
- What's her biggest success at work, and why does she think it happened?
- What's the worst failure at work? And why did that happen? (Is she a victim?)
- Who's the best manager she ever had? And why?
- Who's the worst manager she ever had? And what could that manager have done better to work with her?

Take notes on these answers. Stay present. So when you go back and have that meeting with the other two interviewers, you can have an intelligent conversation. Hire her for the right reasons. Make sure she fits and will be a good investment. When you all three agree that she's a good choice, then it's time to call her references.

You want to discover her strengths and weaknesses from the references. Again, you're still getting a more detailed picture. What impressed them most about her? What are her obstacles? Would they trust her with their wallets or around a special family member? If there's silence at this point, you might want to question your judgment. Put as many details into that picture as you can.

Once the three of you agree this is a good prospect, that this is somebody you can invest in, move to the next step. Give her information that fits her picture. Show her how she'd be crazy to turn you down. You get her. You care. You believe in her. All of you do—she's part of this family. Tell her the hours she'll be working. Explain the benefits package. And finally, go to the third step—offer her solutions with choices. Offer her the job. Show her your commitment, how great this opportunity is for her, and how you will help her achieve her dreams and goals—whatever it takes.

Your job has just begun

Now you must help her succeed. Make her fearless, unstoppable, and bold. You hired a good person, with plenty of drive and enthusiasm. If she doesn't succeed, then it's your fault as a leader, teacher, coach, and role model. Believe in her, and tell her that frequently. Find her gold chain. Set her up so she wins. It's your job as a leader to make it simple and more natural for folks to be comfortable in this business. And that starts with hiring the right people, believing in them, and making good investments.

When I was younger, I thought I was in the wrong business because *it didn't fit*. It turns out, I wasn't in the wrong business; I was *in the business wrong*. When I got in the business right, it was a gold mine. Your job is to make the business feel good by providing employees with a powerfully motivating environment that supports advancement, success, growth, and profitability. Everything has to fit and feel good, so they can be confident and successful and proud! You do that by saying, "I got you. You're going to be successful. I guarantee it."

That's your key to retiring rich—in spirit and in your bank account.

Teaching at desk

As we discussed back in chapter seven, one of our biggest lost opportunities is that managers are rarely taught how to teach effectively at desk. I see this over and over again in dealership after dealership. The salespeople go into a classroom where a teacher, manager, computer program, or consultant teaches them the what, when, and how's of selling. Then the salespeople are supposed to go out and automatically start using whatever techniques or scripts they just learned. In some cases, it's not supported at desk. Your job as a leader is to reinforce and continue teaching whatever they learned in the classroom.

Sometimes it takes a while for people to adopt a new strategy or technique. And if the only place they heard it was in a classroom, the chances they ever actually use it are slim. But if you are at the desk consistently reinforcing the lesson over and over again, they will Get The Picture that this is how things work here now. The Keep It Simple Selling process I outlined is easy, duplicatable, and teachable at desk. You have the opportunity to reinforce the learning every time someone touches desk.

So, when you're teaching, use the framework I've outlined here, and you'll see a marked improvement. Remember, you don't have to change your process. Just chunk it down into the three steps you just learned in chapter 7—Get The Picture, Give Information, and Offer Solutions With Choices. I guarantee your current sales process can be chunked down to those three steps, reinforced, and taught at desk—which will increase your profitability and create lifelong relationships with grateful salespeople.

If you have no idea what I'm selling you right now, go read chapter 7 again. Your people are worth it.

Managers don't yell

If from your salespeople's perspectives, it appears they're being yelled at, you might want to rethink your communication style from an advanced level. When somebody speaks with a lot of volume and uses only one note, it sounds like they're yelling. But if they add a little melody with the volume, it's perceived completely different. You can go to http://AutoTrainingAcademy.com/melody-and-volume/ and hear exactly what I'm talking about. With melody, the voice comes across as passion with volume.

Be patient, and understand that some managers and others in our industry do not communicate at this higher level. They just may have a communication handicap. They come across as angry. As we say in the South, "Bless their hearts, 'cause they just don't talk good."

Managers, you're better than this. You want great salespeople driven to succeed. Be the kind of leader who drives people to achieve their greatest dreams. Treat them like royalty. Respect and recognize them by seeing them at their best. When they don't believe in themselves, believe for them. And try adding some melody to your voice. You might just get better results from your employees. If you choose to hire people who aren't worthy of your attention, respect, and leadership, and you think *they* are the problem—think again.

This is the greatest industry in the world—a gold mine for so many of us. We deserve better leaders, role models, mentors, and coaches. You're an expert at this business, great with people, passionate, driven, and someone saw the good in you. Pass it on. You represent the dreams that are possible in this industry, and you must choose to hire great people that you can invest in fully, with no regret.

Own it!

Okay, it's time to implement what you've learned in this chapter. Fill in the blanks with words from your I AM list.

What qualities, characteristics, and values must I have so that I can recruit, hire, and train great team members? Write your list, and then narrow it down to what will drive you.

I am _____   I am _____

I am _____   I am _____

I am _____   I am _____

I am _____   I am _____

I am _____   I am _____

I am _____   I am _____

I am _____   I am _____

I am _____, _____, and _____ so that _____.

What qualities, characteristics, and values must I have so that I can create and grow an energetic, motivated, driven, and successful sales environment? Write your list, and then narrow it down to what will drive you.

I am _____   I am _____

I am _____   I am _____

I am _____   I am _____

I am _____   I am _____

I am _____   I am _____

I am _____   I am _____

I am _____   I am _____

I am _____   I am _____

I am _____, _____, and _____ so that

_____.

What qualities, characteristics, and values must I have so that I can teach, mentor, role model, and lead in a way that attracts happy, productive, and profitable team members? Write your list, and then narrow it down to what will drive you.

I am _____   I am _____

I am _____   I am _____

I am _____   I am _____

I am _____   I am _____

I am _____   I am _____

I am _____   I am _____

I am _____, _____, and _____ so that

_____.

BREAK THE RULES...WRITE IN THE BOOK!

_____

_____

_____

_____

_____

_____

_____

_____

_____

_____

_____

_____

_____

_____

_____

_____

_____

_____

_____

_____

_____

_____

_____

_____

_____

KEEP IT SIMPLE

This business is a gold mine. It can be all yours, but you've got to dig deep. It takes work to make it incredible. Success in this industry can be simple though—it takes two things:

First, you've got to get good at being you. Know who you are at your best. Know how you're being judged. And talk from your heart so that you're worth listening to.

Second, you've got to take care of people. Love and care for others. Understand that lifelong relationships are the key to this business— relationships built on trust and helping customers find what they want and need. This business is not just about selling a car. It's about solving and serving and being a part of your customers' lives. When you shake someone's hand in person, on the phone, or by email, you've got to maintain that relationship forever.

You can be like the little pig that built an Up business with straw and only sells 20 percent of the people he speaks with. Or you can own a brick-solid business by building and maintaining lifelong relationships and sell 80 percent of the people you visit with. It's your choice. Your raise becomes effective when you do.

You'll also want to create a customer driven process that works naturally for you and is 100 percent honest, so you can treat people like royalty and solve their transportation needs. Your dealership's existing processes can easily be chunked down to three easy-to-remember steps.

Get The Picture—Discover the PP.
Give Information—Based on the picture.
Offer Solutions with choices—Solve the PP.
Use the picture!!!

That's it—a process that works for the entire dealership. It works for salespeople, service advisors, managers, conflict resolution, hiring, Internet—and even works away from the dealership. It's easy to teach, learn, and remember—and it's based on natural behavior. When you were in second grade, you instinctively knew how to sell and close. You were curious, so you asked questions to Get the Picture, and you believed in the deal. Keep it Simple, like a second grader.

Finally, our industry is hungry for great leaders—people who can teach, lead, and mentor. Leaders who recruit, hire, develop, teach, motivate, and guarantee more people success. Find and hire employees who have passion, drive, dreams, and who have a desire to grow and learn. Then teach them how to succeed. We need leaders who will do whatever it takes to make employees' dreams and goals become reality. Invest in your people, and you'll be rewarded beyond measure.

The business of your business is people.

The key to massive success is building and maintaining lifelong relationships.

When you do that, you'll be profitable and proud of what you do.

I am grateful that I found this business. I'm happy to be a car guy. Thank you for studying this book. I wish you massive success and happiness for the rest of your days!

Boudreaux

Keep it Simple Success formula
Get good at being you. Take care of others.

ABOUT THE AUTHOR

"I help you align WHO YOU ARE AT YOUR BEST, with what you do, to solve the customer's transportation needs. WHO YOU ARE IS PERFECT to win at this great business."
—Damian Boudreaux

 Damian Boudreaux is a speaker and teacher for the automotive industry. His 30 years of experience selling, training, consulting, and connecting with auto professionals across the United States, South America, and Canada is the perfect recipe for those who are hungry to improve every area of their lives. He educates and inspires folks

to succeed by believing in themselves, the deal, their product, their company and their service—one lifelong relationship at a time.

Damian started out cleaning parts in his friend's transmission shop. From there, he tried and stumbled and tried again to sell more cars than the month before. It wasn't until he began to open his eyes and pay attention to the people around him that he understood what it really takes to succeed in the automotive business. The lessons he learned during his journey to becoming a top-selling salesman are humbling and inspiring at the same time. Damian compares stumbling into the auto industry to winning the mega-million jackpot. It's a gold mine, and an amazing journey.

Damian's unique approach to relationship selling has helped thousands of salespeople, service advisors, managers, and dealers double their dollars in this business. Every business connected to the automotive industry can benefit from Damian's techniques and strategies. His perspective makes our industry simple, noble, profitable, and fun!

"In the more than 40 years I have worked with trainers and speakers throughout the automotive business like Jackie B. Cooper, Grant Cardone, Joe Girard, Clint McGhee, Jim Zeigler, Tom Stuker as well as legendary speakers such as Dr. Norman Vincent Peale, Dr. Robert Schuller, Dr. Wayne Dyer, Paul Harvey, J. Douglas Edwards, Zig Ziglar and many more...**Damian's unique way of teaching people in the automotive industry is brilliant. His ability to communicate and connect, along with his simple techniques about relationship selling, solving, and serving is exactly what people need to be successful and proud of what they do every day.**"

—**Bob Mohr**, President of Mohr & Associates

WITH LOVE FOR:

Nichole, Anna Louise, Andrea (Andi), and Monique

With Gratitude:

The Miracle Foundation is a trusted, international, non-profit organization that believes children can and should be lifted out of the cycle of poverty.

THE MIRACLE FOUNDATION

WWW.MIRACLEFOUNDATION.ORG

We partner with struggling orphanages to feed, clothe, nourish, and educate their children. Through years of experience, we have found that the most powerful way to help people help themselves is to strengthen existing orphanages and transform them into loving homes where children can thrive. This approach empowers caregivers and children.

It's transforming. It's measurable. It's proven. It's scalable, and it's just an awesome thing to do.

Join us on this journey at www.MiracleFoundation.org

ACKNOWLEDGEMENTS

Whether you know it or not, you had a huge part in the making of this book.

Thank you!

Special thanks to my inspirational and supportive family: Robert and Leneta, Jerry and Theresa, Alyce-Elise, Anne, Douglas, Claire, Caroline, Andre, and their families.

Mentors who passed away too soon: Red Hickman, Sid Guidroz, W. C. Johnson, Dick Yax, Ron Hoffman, Tom Bessett, Ray Willig, Ramsey Gillman, Leo Jarnagin, Ivan Tufty, Henry Adams, Leonard Edwards, and Michelle Bono.

Special thanks to: Bob Mohr, Julie Anne Eason, Willie S. King Jr., Jerry Cousin, Greg Gaspard, George Armstrong, Betty Raglin, Roger Simmons, Larry Barker, Gary Avery, Tracey Charlebois, Bjorn Allpas, Stacy Gillman, Jason Gillman, Chris Gillman, Patrick York, Rasool Rastgoo, Ronnie Bernal, Scott Dupons, Jay Gould, Brad Mugg, Richard Fisler, Steve Kubitz, Scott Montgomery, Ruthie Keene, Don Davis, Terryl DeCuire, Doug McClanahan, Lee Beaman, Ann Eaden, Carl Heflin,

Steve Kash, Carolyn Cross, Tom Pearce, Scott Morgan, Grant Cardone, Jenni Robbins, Brendon Burchard, Mel Abraham, Roger Love, Bo Eason, Jack Guarrity, Jack Sherrod, Bob Brockman, Mike Allessi, Trey Hiers, Dan Agan, Tony Fowler, Mike Willis, David DeLuz Jr., Darryl Turner, Matt O'Daniel, Tony Swindell, Mike Van Ryn, Tony Ciaravino, Johnny DeArmond, Darryl Landry, Dan Creamer, Shane Dodson, Carl Jones, Mike Good, David Baker, Fred Price, Ralph Mahalak, Gil Yale, Bill Willis, Skip Willis, Nick Luppino, Chris Snellgrove, Darren Gordon, Gary Hudgins, David Tucker, John Kostakis, J. R. Caporal, Mark Kolon, Mario DelBosque, David Kemp, Lane Tokunaga, Neil Crain, Michael Hunter, Rick Frishman, Scott Hoffman, Terry Whalin, and David Hancock.

CPSIA information can be obtained at www.ICGtesting.com
Printed in the USA
BVOW05s1554250815

414944BV00006B/147/P